On Their Own?

*Making the Transition from
School to Work in the Information Age*

The job market in Canada has changed dramatically in the last fifteen years. Improvements in technology allow business to do more with less labour and to demand higher education levels and more technical skills for entry-level jobs. Youth unemployment has remained high since the 1982 recession. Transition to work is one of the toughest challenges facing Canadian youth in the information age but *On Their Own* can help make the passage smooth and successful.

Using samples of young adults in four urban centres, parents, former teachers, and employers, the authors identify the factors that ease transition from school to work. These include level of education, social class, gender, ethnicity, aspirations of parents, help from role models, participation in co-op education, and most important of all, self-motivation. The authors describe a range of profiles – uncommitted, non-careerists, conservatives, and innovators – that will help youth, parents, and educators promote a successful move into the workplace.

Emphasizing the importance of cooperative education, the authors suggest that closer relations between school and work, such as those found in the United Kingdom and Sweden, facilitate transition into the labour market. *On Their Own* will guide parents, youth, educators, trustees, employers, and ministries of education and training to prepare a new generation of productive, resilient workers and managers for the information age.

STEWART CRYSDALE, professor emeritus and senior scholar, York University, is known internationally for innovative work in transition. He is a past president of the Canadian Sociology and Anthropology Association.

ALAN J.C. KING is a leading researcher in education and past director of the Social Programs Evaluation Group, Queen's University.

NANCY MANDELL, a specialist in family and feminism studies, is former director of the Centre for Feminist Research, York University.

On Their Own?

Making the Transition
from School to Work
in the Information Age

STEWART CRYSDALE,
ALAN J.C. KING, and
NANCY MANDELL

WITH DAVID N. ASHTON,
RUNE AXELSSON, and ERIK WALLIN

McGill-Queen's University Press
Montreal & Kingston · London · Ithaca

© McGill-Queen's University Press 1999
ISBN 0-7735-1785-5 (cloth)
ISBN 0-7735-1805-3 (paper)

Legal deposit first quarter 1999
Bibliothèque nationale du Québec

Printed in Canada on acid-free paper

This book has been published with the help
of a grant from the Humanities and
Social Sciences Federation of Canada, using funds
provided by the Social Sciences and
Humanities Research Council of Canada.

McGill-Queen's University Press acknowledges
the financial support of the Government of Canada
through the Book Publishing Industry Development Program for its activities. We also acknowledge the support
of the Canada Council for the Arts
for our publishing program.

Photos: Students at Seneca College (Stewart Crysdale)

Canadian Cataloguing in Publication Data

Crysdale, Stewart, 1914–
On their own?: making the transition from
school to work in the information age
Includes bibliographical references and index.
ISBN 0-7735-1785-5 (bound)
ISBN 0-7735-1805-3 (pbk.)
1. School-to-work transition–Canada. 2.Youth–
Employment–Canada. I. King, Alan J. C., 1933–
II. Mandell, Nancy III. Title.
HD6276.C32C79 1999   331.3′4′0971   C98-901356-1

This book was typeset by Typo Litho Composition
Inc. in 10.5/13 Baskerville.

Dedicated with love and gratitude to our spouses, children, and grandchildren.

Church-related teenagers at Kawagana Lake weekend, Ontario. Stewart Crysdale is at the centre of the front row.

Contents

Figures and Tables

Preface and
Acknowledgments

This study focuses on two problems. First, why are so many young people having such a stormy time finding permanent jobs in a growing economy? Since the 1982 recession, global competition for markets has greatly increased, accented by free trade and the spread of new technologies. Companies are cutting staff and computerizing to boost profits. Most new jobs require post-secondary education, which most youth do not have.

Second, what can be done to ease youth's transition into work? To answer this question we first have to learn what helps and what hinders. As it stands, most youth are left on their own to find the way.

Unemployment among those under 25 in 1982 leaped to 18.7 percent and has remained high – 17.0 percent for those between 15 and 24 in January, 1997, compared with 8.4 percent among men over 24 and 8.2 for women (Statistics Canada 1997). Actual numbers are higher since many have given up looking. Discouraged, they leave school early. Undereducated and without experience, their prospects are dark (Organization for Economic Co-operation and Development [OECD] 1996A and B; Bruce Little 1995A and B; 1996).

Youth must brace against the powerful cross-currents of social class, gender, ethnicity, education that often seems apart from real life, and a stringent labour market. Governments prop up parts of the system piecemeal for the short term, but major integrating changes are needed.

This study builds on the design and findings of a pioneering 16-year project, started in 1969, in working-class "Eastside," downtown Toronto (Crysdale and MacKay 1994). Like that study, this one sees transition whole, as youth experience it. We hope that the study will help the main players – youth, parents, teachers, and employers – to act together in easing youth's entrance into the work world.

Our methods combine statistical analysis with case studies to show how the game is won or lost. Compelling evidence is generated to point in directions change should take. The search for that evidence is the motif of the book.

The authors shared fully in the design and development of the project. Nancy Mandell drew on her special knowledge of family and gender in Canada to guide chapter 3 and Alan King's familiarity with secondary and co-op education provided a base for chapters 4 and 5. Stewart Crysdale directed the fieldwork and analysis and drafted most of the manuscript. He also took pictures of students and instructors at Seneca College of Applied Arts and Technology, Toronto, by permission and with the assistance of Laura Mandell.

The Social Sciences and Humanities Research Council of Canada furnished grants over four years. The senior author is also indebted to the Small Grants and Teaching Development Committees at York University, the Scandinavian Studies Foundation, and the University of Reading and Uppsala University for support during a visit to Europe in 1992.

Atkinson College, the Institute for Social Research at York University, through John Tibert, and the Social Programs Evaluation Group at Queen's University contributed technical backup. The project was also supported through the Kitty Lundy Memorial Fund and Crysdale's generic research grant. Versions of the study were presented by the senior author at conferences of the Canadian Sociology and Anthropology Association at Brock University and the American Sociology Association in Toronto, both in 1997, and at five provincial and national meetings of Cooperative Education associations in 1995 and 1996.

Area consultants Arden Walther at the University of Ottawa, Sid Gilbert at Guelph, and Ibrahim Alladin at Alberta gave valuable leadership. So did field coordinators Lisbeth Donaldson, now at Calgary, Rose Hutcheon at York, Carol Thibault at Ottawa, and Danny Zabelishensky at Guelph. Outstanding among interviewers were Janice Joseph, Christine Lynch, Eugene Spanier, Mary

Power, Romi Malik, Andrew Kerr-Wilson, Deborah Cope, Michael MacKay, Dana Carswell, Abinash Mishra, Kathleen Fincham, Patty Spittal, Lith Kobbekadai, Rita Niekamp, Maryanne Hodgeson, and Gulshaw Merchant.

Hazel O'Loughlin-Vidal, Heather Spurll, Rita Marinucci, Joy Thomas, and Agnes Fraser skillfully processed drafts and Joanne Close improved the text. Ministry of Education officials in Alberta and Ontario, administrators in four school boards, and teams of phone canvassers located the sample. Anonymous reviewers criticized drafts and editors improved the text. Finally, the goodwill and openness of 1,003 interviewees and respondents gave the project life. We hope that the results justify their trust.

On Their Own?

CHAPTER ONE

Introduction

The purposes of this study may be expressed in four questions:

1 What opportunities are there for youth to prepare for productive and gratifying employment?
2 How do youth respond?
3 What are the effects of class, gender, ethnicity, and personal goals and values?
4 How might controlling structures be changed to widen opportunities and motivate youth?

We join the search for ways to smooth youth's journey from home and school into work. Young people enter a maze where taking a false turn could mean a lifetime of disadvantage. Many leave school without a certificate, beginning a life of haphazard, depressed employment. Even graduates experience difficulty in finding permanent, full-time jobs (Ontario Premier's Council 1988; Karp 1988; Radwanski 1987; Donaldson 1989; Krahn and Lowe 1991; Sunter 1993, 1994; Crysdale and MacKay 1994). Success in transition to work, according to Statistics Canada, depends on varied factors such as field and level of study, age, work experience, social status of family, initiative, area of residence, and economic conditions (Don Little 1995).

When the 324 young adults in our sample left high school in the mid-1980s, an estimated 30 percent of their cohorts across the country were dropouts. Six years later, in a large survey of 18- to 20-year-olds, Statistics Canada found that the proportion without a diploma had declined to 18 percent (Gilbert et al. 1993). What was happening?

More young people are staying in school and many of the jobless are returning to the classroom (Statistics Canada 1996). New jobs call for more education and technical expertise. Besides, cooperative education and partnerships are spreading, linking education with employment (Conference Board of Canada 1995B). Early school leaving still imprints ugly social and psychological scars (Gilbert et al. 1993; Tanner et al. 1995; Burman 1988). Many leavers lack the skills and will to re-enter school. In 1992 191,000 youth under the age of 25 were neither in school nor in the labour force. A quarter of them believed that searching for work was futile; that no jobs were open to them. They lacked post-secondary education; many had dropped out of school (Sunter 1993, 1994). The proportion not in school or at work has fallen in recent years for complex reasons. It's both pull and push. Youth continue in school or return to qualify for available jobs. They also go back because they can't find satisfactory work (Krahn and Lowe 1991).

About half our sample had been unemployed, on average for over two months and over a quarter for more than four months. It is surprising that in an affluent society the biggest worry is to find a satisfying job (Bibby and Posterski 1992; Environics 1995).

There's more bad news, though for some it has a silver lining. Half of Canada's high school graduates lack the skills needed for technical jobs, which now account for most new openings (Dodge 1981; Economic Council of Canada 1982; OECD 1996A, vols. 1, 2). The silver lining is that new jobs are multiplying rapidly in the new economy for those with adequate education, training, and *experience* (Bruce Little 1995 A, B). A minority of those under 25 meet all these requirements.

To remedy this dilemma, basic structural changes are needed to bridge the gap between education and employment. Are Canadians ready for these changes? Two-thirds of teachers and parents in this study are. The public also seems favourably disposed (cf. Lewington 1995).

Basic values in Canada strike a balance between individual rights and equalitarian obligations. Given an understanding of the situation, most Canadians approve of widening the chances for youth. A solid majority of the public, along with decision makers, favour a strong role for government in providing for such socioeconomic needs as job training (Ekos Research Associates 1995).

Most Canadians approve of an open mix of subcultures. Women and minorities are challenging the old dominance of WASPS – white Anglo-Saxon Protestant males. Canadian "people openness" ranks above average in the World Competitiveness Report – eighth among 22 industrial countries (Drohan 1997; cf. Peters 1995).

A high rate of selective immigration is renewing the labour force with enterprise and flexibility. Newcomers, especially from the Orient and East Asia, understand the linkage between education and careers, work harder than others, seek more education and are more family-oriented (Statistics Canada 1994B; Beiser et al. 1994; DeVoretz 1995).

The need for change is dramatized by the loss of hundreds of thousands of unskilled and semi-skilled jobs at low-tech levels in manufacturing, clerical, and general service work. The shift to high-tech employment heightens demand for closer relations between education and work. And the push for more regional/provincial control of the economy, as in training, could facilitate reforms in preparing youth for employment.

The explosion of information and communication technology affects the intrinsic nature of work, stressing abstract reasoning and developing new skills (OECD 1994). New technology spread rapidly in the 1970s and 1980s but growth has slowed as individuals, firms, and governments adjust. Canada was a leader in the 1980s but we have fallen behind, for example, in the proportion of research and development personnel in the total workforce, ranking 13 out of 22 members of the OECD in 1991 (ibid. 1994:128; OECD 1996A, 2:20). Nor has Canada's productivity growth matched that in some countries (Conference Board of Canada 1997). Employment growth in high technology business has been strong but not in the overall labour market.

The situation of unskilled workers has deteriorated while the earnings of those able to use new technologies have risen considerably. This fosters a "duality between info-connected haves and info-excluded have-nots" (OECD 1996A, 1:25). Polarization of income from wages and salaries has been eased by public support in western Europe and in Canada but in the US and Mexico it has been allowed to soar (Riddell 1995).

However, because of pressure in world markets, reduction of the workforce through technology, and trimming of social support, particularly by Ottawa and Ontario, poverty has mounted rapidly in Canadian cities. For example, between 1990 and 1995 the number of children depending on welfare in greater Toronto rose from 18 to 33.4 percent, bringing the total to 100,000 youngsters (Metropolitan Toronto Social Planning Council 1996). The main cause of increased poverty is the precarious labour market. More workers at low-skill jobs are earning less because they can find only part-time or seasonal jobs. In 1995 5,205,000 Canadians lived in poverty – 17.8 percent, compared with 17.1 percent in 1994 (Caledon Institute of Social Policy 1996). The key policy issue, according to the OECD, is for governments to balance the economic need to upgrade production through technology with the social need to broaden opportunities to share in benefits. This balance can be furthered by reforming education from elementary grades up, improving transition to work, retraining, and lifelong learning (OECD 1996B, 23).

One cogent feature of the technologized world market is the heightened demand for literacy in reading skill, in handling documents, and in calculating numbers. This demand must be met by families, schools, and businesses, though the heaviest burden falls on education. More education raises the level of literacy – and employment potential. An analysis of the International Adult Literacy Survey of 1994 compares the performance of Canada with six trading partners (Canada, Ministry of Industry 1996). Canadians compare well with some others at high job levels but are far behind the Swedes. At the middle level we are surpassed by Germany, the Netherlands, Sweden, and Switzerland. The United States is close behind Canada. Comparisons at the top levels are drawn in Table 1-1.

Fifty to 55 percent of professionals in Canada score in the top half of literacy scales. They are followed closely by technicians, managers, and officials. Then at much lower levels come those at clerical, service, and sales jobs. At the bottom are craft and machine workers, clustered at literacy levels 1 and 2. "If skilled craft jobs are essential to a high-skill, high-wage economy Canada lags behind its major competitors ... Steps must be taken to improve both the skills of employees and the literacy opportunities in the workplace" (ibid., 61).

Table 1–1

Literacy at Top Occupational Levels, Seven Countries, Ages 16–65* (Percentages)

	Literacy Scales		
	Prose	Documents	Numbers
Canada	33	25	22
Germany	13	19	24
Netherlands	15	20	20
Poland	3	6	7
Sweden	32	36	36
Switzerland	10	16	20
United States	21	19	23

* Based on Table 1.3 in Canada, Minister of Industry and Statistics, 1996.

THEORIES OF TRANSITION AND A HOLISTIC DEVELOPMENTAL MODEL

Seeing the process whole implies a theory of interaction between youth and the main agents of socialization into work – family, school, and workplace. These exert power in two ways: directly, as established organizations with goals and the regimen to achieve them, and indirectly through widely accepted norms of behaviour.

The notion of a holistic developmental design, which would include, simultaneously and by stages, the roles of the individual, family, school, and work, was devised in a longitudinal action-research project conducted from the 1960s to the 1980s by Crysdale and MacKay (1994). The project was longitudinal in that the sample were followed through 16 years in several interviews. It was action-research in that an experimental subgroup were involved in transitional programs and their attainments compared with those of a matching control group who were not involved. The design was tested again in a pilot study for this project with 50 young adults in Peel County in 1988 and applied in subsequent field observations. Now the Organization for Economic Cooperation and Development recommends a holistic-type model to guide governments, educators, employers, and others in developing programs to smooth youth's transition into work. "In a rapidly changing world a strategy for lifelong learning involves many participants and requires a rethinking of roles and responsibilities. Governments in partnership with learners, their families, public and private [employers], teachers [and other agencies, including unions and social services bodies] are best placed to set the policy framework for developing systems and networks through which individuals learn" (OECD 1996B, 23).

Built into the design are youth's perceptions of their own future roles and of the aspirations influential others hold for them. Hence, to use Weber's classic distinction, interaction may create both mechanical and organic solidarity or integration between the novice and the institutions with which he or she deals (Weber 1958).

This scheme draws particularly on critical theory, where a measure of conflict between players, as individuals and groups, is endemic in the struggle for power (Collins 1988, ch. 8). Interaction with groups may lead the entrant to recognize legitimate authority on the part of family, school, and business but to question power wielded arbitrarily through class, gender, or ethnicity (Coleman 1990).

We also draw on social learning theory, which relates the individual reciprocally with both influential others and the socioeconomic and cultural environment (Bandura 1971). When there is reciprocity, cooperation, and consonance, transitional outcomes are apt to be positive.

Our case studies illustrate at a microlevel how "symbolic interaction" binds youth and influential others together through common goals and appropriate behavioural patterns.

The model in Figure 1-1 provides for the systematic analysis of transitional interaction. It specifies relevant variables by stages in youth's journey and allows the measurement of relations between "causes" and outcomes. It is holistic, including broad structures and individual values and actions. The model is also developmental; variables are introduced in the order in which they usually occur.

While structures exercise powerful control, individuals in democracies may resist and follow their own course. Many youth ignore elders and celebrate their sixteenth birthday by simply walking out of school (Ontario, Ministry of Education 1988; Ontario, Ministry of Skills Development 1987, 1988; Gilbert et al. 1993).

A	B	C	D
Background	*Early Experiences*	*Intermediate Factors*	*Outcomes*
Structural	*Structural*	*Structural*	*Structural*
Youth's social class measured by parents' education and occupation	Parents' aspirations for youth's education and occupation	Consonance among elders' views on democratic decision making – educational and occupational goals separately	Youth's present full-time job
			Steady employment
Youth's ethnicity (Race is not taken into account due to insufficient numbers for significant analysis.)	Teachers' aspirations for youth's education and occupation		Pay, full time
			On-the-job training, length
	Employers' aspirations for youth's education and occupation	Consonance in overall total views of elders on decision making and goals for youth	*Individual*
Gender			Youth's education*
	Participation in work education (co-op) at high school	School's view of purpose of education	Intrinsic job satisfaction
Help from mothers, fathers, peers, and teachers			Innovative career planning
	*Individual***	*Individual*	
	Effort at school	Gender equality score	
	Average marks	Efficacy of beliefs	
	Youth's job aspirations	Religious practice	

Figure 1–1   A Holistic Stage Model of Transition[+]

[+] The time-span in this model begins in about Grade Nine, when youth are about 15 years old, and continues until their mid-twenties. Our youth sample are a cohort group who recall their experiences during this period, approximately from 1980 to 1990.

[*] Youth's present education, for the majority, is something they cannot or will not change and in this sense is structural. However, a minority may return for further education or training.

[**] Variables labelled "Individual" signify a large measure of choice for youth, whereas "structural" signifies little opportunity for choice, as perceived by youth in their mid-twenties at the time of interview.

We will measure the strength of relationships between antecedent factors and each of seven dimensions of transition, using at
first cross-tabulations and correlations. In chapter 8 we will com-
pute the impact of antecedents on outcomes simultaneously, using multiple regression tables. In multiple regression computer
formulas permit the ranking of the impact of defined preceding
factors on important outcomes, according to their strength.

Three obvious dimensions of transition are *levels of education, position,* and *pay.* There is also *steady work* in contrast to unemployment. *Job training* may lead to promotion, security, and prestige
(Evers 1990; Canadian Labour Market Productivity Centre 1988).
Intrinsic job satisfaction signifies satisfaction with work tasks in
themselves in contrast to extrinsic satisfaction that derives from
wages, security, and working conditions (Deci 1972; King et al.
1979; Kohn 1976; Ninalowo 1983). The final dimension is *innovativeness* in career planning, which indicates that a worker pre-
fers jobs that change and require continual retraining.

An important lever for positive transition is the type of *work education* a student may take. Some programs are short, without experience on the job, while others constitute a full course and involve
the student in supervised tasks at a workplace. We expected that
the latter – "cooperative," or "work experience," programs – are
more helpful.

The model in Figure 1-1 guides what follows through the book.
Under "stage" A background factors are listed. Those that are
structural include social class, ethnicity, and gender, while individual factors may include help from mother, father, peers, and
teachers.

In stage B early experiences include structural factors such as
aspirations for schooling and jobs that are held for youth by parents, teachers, and employers, along with participation in work
education (Woelfel and Haller 1971; D.L. Thomas 1974). Also
several individual factors come to bear: effort at school, average
marks, and youth's job aspirations.

Other less direct intermediate factors – stage C – enter the process at this point as well. These include consonance or consistency
in the hopes of elders for youth's education and occupation.[1] We
also consider the impact of individual beliefs or values. These include gender equality norms, efficacy of beliefs, and religious
practice.

Stage D lists major outcomes or dimensions of transition: education and full-time job levels, steady employment, pay, on-the-job training, intrinsic job satisfaction, and innovative career planning. These individual factors are affected by preceding structural variables and also have a reciprocal impact on them.

A COMPARATIVE PERSPECTIVE

We can understand transition in Canada better if we compare it with the process in the United Kingdom and Sweden, described in chapter 9. Though different from each other, their systems are more orderly than ours, and both are centrally or institutionally oriented. The UK has a tiered system in which students at entrance to high school are streamed according to standing in national exams. Placement in Sweden, with its equalitarian values, is delayed until Grade Twelve, when students select a specialized upper-school program from 16 lines, 14 of which are applied (OECD 1995). Compared with Canada, a smaller minority in both the UK and Sweden go on directly to university; most head for specialized business or trade programs at the secondary or college levels.

In Canadian education there is a stubborn anomaly. On one hand a very high proportion of age cohorts graduate from university – 38 percent (just under the United States' 39 percent), compared with 29 percent in the UK and 15 percent in Sweden. On the other hand, Canada stands third lowest among 19 OECD countries in secondary school completion – 68 percent of the age cohort, as against 76 percent in the US, 80 percent in the UK, and 82 percent in Sweden (OECD 1996B: 66, 65). In both the UK and Sweden employers are fully involved in education, training, and counselling.

In Canada and the US there is a widening gap between the haves and have-nots, beginning with education and training (Morissette et al. 1995, 23). This is aggravated by the general downgrading of young workers under 25 in spite of their higher educational attainment compared with other workers. They are downgraded partly because of inexperience and lack of seniority. Their elders are firmly established in a range of positions, often protected by collective bargaining or employment contracts. To a larger degree now than in 1981, those under 25 who are in full-time jobs are paid less per hour than those with seniority. In 1991 dollars wages fell by 14 percent for young men and 12 percent for young women between 1981 and 1988, whereas for those aged 55 to 64 they increased by 15 percent for men and remained the same for older women (ibid. 1995).

THE SAMPLE AREAS AND YOUTH PROFILE

Interviews were conducted with a sample of 324 young adults in their mid-twenties who, five years earlier (1984–85), had left ten high schools, some with and some without a diploma, in four metro areas: Peel, which is in the Toronto basin, Guelph and Ottawa in Ontario, and Edmonton in Alberta. These were suggested by Education ministry officials as being typical of high schools in working/middle-class areas that offered co-op education. With minor regional differences, sample youth were subject to a more or less ubiquitous metropolitan culture. The relative homogeneity of the area youth in mean outcomes warrants their being treated as one sample. Because of the selection process, sample youth surpass national averages in social class and attainments.

As their school records were five years old, we could not find many of the youth in the sample frame. Of those who could be found, we visited 89 percent at home or work and conducted our 324 interviews, which averaged an hour and a half. We also gathered data through interviews with the parents of 115 of the youth and through questionnaires answered by 287 former teachers and 277 employers. All in all, 1,003 people were involved in the study.

Fifty-five percent of the youth sample were women; they are more accessible for interviewing. Sixty percent of the parents we contacted were Anglo-Saxon. This includes a few of French origin since their views are similar. Almost one-third were of other European extraction, while most of the remainder were of Oriental or East Asian origin. Fourteen percent of sample youth did not complete a secondary program, 29 percent completed high school or took courses at community college, 18 percent finished college, and 38 percent had taken some university courses, graduated, or were still students. If the somewhat privileged youth in the sample had problems in transition, those of lower socioeconomic status and fewer opportunities can be expected to have even greater difficulty.

Our interviewees mentioned structural obstacles to a smooth transition. These included inequality of opportunity arising from class, gender, and ethnicity; gulfs between families and school and between school and work; mixed signals or none at all from influential others; separation between applied and academic programs; the lack of on-the-job training and the jurisdictional split between provinces and the federal state, the former controlling education and the latter training.

These and other issues are addressed in what follows, beginning with emerging experiences in chapter 2 and the impact of family status, gender and ethnicity in chapter 3. Then we examine correlates of education in chapter 4, cooperative education in chapter 5, and work in chapter 6. A new factor is the topic of chapter 7 – the bearing on outcomes of consonance in others' hopes for youth. In chapter 8 we compare the weights of various antecedents on specified outcomes. Because of smoother transition to the workplace in the UK and Sweden, we examine their systems in chapter 9 through contributed articles. Finally, we present a summary of findings and conclusions in chapter 10.

CHAPTER TWO

Along the Way:
Emerging Experiences

EXPERIENCES, ASPIRATIONS, AND HELP

Sequential change is normal in nature and society. In this chapter we trace sequences of structural and individual factors midway in youth's transition to work and conclude with a typology of youth's journey based on their own accounts.

Early experiences, as outlined in stage B of the model in Figure 1–1, include structural factors such as the aspirations of influential others and participation in work education. These are structural in that they are part of systems that are largely out of the control of youth. Experiences also include individual factors such as effort at school, marks, and expectations for jobs ten years hence. Intermediate experiences, shown in stage C, are broader. Structural factors there include youth's participation in decision making and consonance or consistency in elders' aspirations for them. Individual factors at stage C express values such as flexibility in gender norms, efficacy of beliefs, and religious practice.

Youth tend to internalize the aspirations influential people hold for them as authoritative signals of their future. The small minority who take co-op education also build goals partly on what they learn from co-op personnel.

Eighty-seven percent of the youth in our sample said that they received clear messages from their parents about educational goals. Over half of the parents wanted their children to go through university – an unrealistic dream for many. Forty percent of the youth did not know what teachers hoped for them and fewer still knew what employers hoped.

Mothers gave the most support (as rated by 63 percent of youth) through setting goals and in practical ways, followed by fathers (53 percent) and peers (41 percent). Only 34 percent said that teachers had supported them strongly during the transition from school to work. Nearly 80 percent of youth said that they themselves were mostly responsible.

Girls rated teachers' hopes for their education a little higher than boys did. Youth whose parents had the best jobs rated help from teachers lower than others did; the expectations of these parents were high. Parents with higher-than-average status serve as primary models for their children and have more resources than others to guide them. Their children tend to have more self-confidence.

Former co-op students gave the highest scores for teachers' help and credited parents with help more than non-co-op students did. As chapter 5 shows, co-op programs were found to be important in setting goals and stimulating performance.

MARKS AND EFFORT AT SCHOOL

Average marks and effort in the last year of high school are shown in Table 2–1. Amount of effort, an unusual statistic, proved to be extremely helpful in understanding transition. Almost half of our sample youth admitted that they coasted through school.

Youth from Oriental and East Indian minorities generally made a stronger effort than native-born Anglo- or Francophones. Their ambition, inspired by parents whose own educational status was in many cases low, more than compensated for linguistic problems. They also got better marks and went further than most Anglo-Saxons (Richmond and Kalback 1980; Reiz 1980; Herberg 1982; Isajiw et al. 1993; Statistics Canada 1994B). Girls in the study worked harder than boys and won better marks in upper school. Their estimate of self-help, or the extent to which their own efforts had helped them to succeed, was also higher.

Help from teachers' in making the transition to work, as reported by former students, is not correlated with marks, probably because students took that help for granted. On the other hand, parental help could not be assumed. When it was extraordinary it was acknowledged by youth.

Table 2–1
Marks and Self-Report of Effort at High School (Percentages)

Marks		Effort at School	
Under 60	6	Very little	23
60–69	33	Less than best	22
70–79	44	Moderate effort	37
80–93	17	Great effort	16
Total	100	Total	98
Frequencies	(319)	Frequencies	(310)

For most students, effort was correlated positively with marks. Being bright, having a good memory, even high parental status, in themselves were not enough. Striving made the critical difference.

Positive participation in the co-op program on the whole did not affect marks. This does not discredit co-op. On the contrary, it means that co-op students in our sample, who were drawn heavily from disprivileged families, made a greater effort than others and attained average grades.

HOPES, REALITY, AND JOBS

Young adults in their mid-twenties have unrealistic career hopes. Only two percent of those in our study expected to end up in un-skilled or semi-skilled jobs; in fact, 35 percent did. Half thought they would be managers of mid-size or large firms, owners, or professionals; only seven percent attained such levels. Thirty per-cent of parents shared their children's unlikely dreams (see Table A–1).

Judging from the parents' present positions, there is room at the upper levels for only one-quarter of the new generation. Al-though the sample was above national averages in terms of educa-tion and occupation, the optimism of our subjects was misplaced. Some young adults will work their way up – 11 percent were still in post-secondary education when interviewed. When they are added to the seven percent already in relatively high position, 18 percent have good prospects. In this respect teachers' expecta-tions are right on – 19 percent.

Few teachers, however, talked about prospects in skilled trades. Still fewer employers talked about careers with young workers; among those who did, only eight percent encouraged youth to go for high positions.

Nearly half of parents, nearly two-thirds of teachers, and almost as many employers said nothing at all to students about careers. Some said, "It's up to them," or "We don't want to impose our ideas on them."

Actually, 31 percent of our sample youth worked at the skilled level, compared with the 25 percent who thought they would be there ten years hence. Eleven percent were supervisors or managers of small units. Yet among parents and employers only 17 percent had hoped the young people would become skilled workers – considerably short of reality. Only five percent of teachers talked about this level as a goal for youth.

Table A–2 provides evidence of the effect of socioeconomic status on youth's efforts and marks. Mothers' job level has a stronger effect than fathers'. Minority ethnicity slightly affects marks and in finer analysis we learned, as stated, that youth from Oriental and Asian origins surpass most others in transitional outcomes, with the exception of jobs. This will be discussed in chapter 6.

THE IMPACT OF VALUES

Earlier studies have shown that values and beliefs affect a wide range of attitudes and behaviour (Rokeach 1973; Bibby and Posterski 1992; Crysdale and MacKay 1994). Our findings show that they have significant effects on effort and attainment (see Table A–3).

One-quarter of the youth sample say that they practise their beliefs and values very little at work. But the remainder say they usually do (60 percent) or sometimes (15 percent). Youth who practise beliefs and values at work tend systematically and slightly more than others to be achievers, winning higher marks at school, getting better pay, and anticipating intrinsic satisfaction in expected jobs.

Overarching religious beliefs are historically and currently related to patterns of behaviour in every aspect of life. Four out of five of the national population, adults and youth, hold traditional views about God and Jesus Christ (Bibby and Posterski 1992;

Angus Reid Group 1993; Posterski 1995). Characteristically, however, two-thirds of youth are not actively involved in religious organizations, which they regard as adult-directed. Their leisure time is usually spent in youth-centred activities in which they attempt to build identities strongly allied with peers.

One-third of our youth sample say that they attend services of worship regularly (18 percent) or occasionally (14 percent). There are significant correlations between regular worship and marks at school, efficacy of beliefs at work and anticipated intrinsic job satisfaction. Youth who attend religious services are also more generally satisfied at work than others (Table A–3; cf. Bibby and Posterski 1985).

Attendance at worship seems to reinforce norms through intergenerational bonding. These norms include commitment, consistent effort, and inner discipline, which are conducive to positive transition. The comparative strength of these and other antecedents of positive transition is tested in chapter 8.

YOUTH'S VIEWS ON CAREERS

When invited youth to describe their transition to work, the youth in our sample expressed four main positions: uncommitted, non-careerist, conservative, and innovative. Most youth belonged to the two latter types, the largest number (38 percent) having innovative attitudes.

Typologies, especially for youth, must be tentative, as people may change their views with the passage of time and the rise of new circumstances. But in the study of transition, typologies are helpful in two ways. They document individual characteristics that affect goals and routes leading towards them. They also provide cues for intervention to help youth prepare for productive and gratifying careers.

Uncommitted   A young woman was uncommitted to a career while in high school and still takes this position. She adapts well to work but finds it boring. She had little support at home and school.

I was never prepared to go to work. I come from a broken home which was difficult as neither parent ever had the time to get involved with what I was doing at school. I took things into my own hands.

I never studied. I was bright but lacked discipline. Socializing after school was much more important than studying. It's not that I couldn't do the work. I just didn't bother.

At Grade Eight a program was introduced where the girls could take shops. I was the only one who did. This I carried through to high school where I decided to be an auto mechanic. (Despite boredom and lack of interest at school, I always vowed that if I never achieved anything else, I would at least get my Grade Twelve diploma.)

Once again, I was the only girl in these shops – woodworking, machining, engines and electricity. These I carried through to Grade Ten. Then I was informed that to be a mechanic you need other courses. So I dropped the machine and wood shops and added auto electricity and science.

I really enjoyed these classes but flunked more than anything. Blame this on lack of studying and discipline. It was more fun going outside with the guys to play handball during class. The teachers knew but said that if you don't do the work you are to blame for failing.

By Grade Eleven I realized that I probably would not become a mechanic. I put myself into an all-girls auto class and dropped the rest of my shops. I also took a personal typing class.

We were offered job placement for a week. I would have loved to be put into an auto shop to get first-hand experience, but they stuck me in an office. A very boring office with five people. This was based on one personal typing course. I was so mad! They didn't even ask where or what type of work you wished to do. They just stuck you in somewhere – anywhere. I didn't learn one thing except that I hate working in offices.

Today I'm an executive secretary and I still hate working in offices. I acquired all my experience on the job. I learn fast but a good description of a secretary is a "glorified babysitter." I feel trapped. I move from one secretarial job to another, but I'm not interested. And I don't want to go back to school either. I'm not really interested in a career because I would like to have a family more than anything else.

Non-careerist This youth recognizes the importance of a career but is still not sure of what it may be. Again there was a gap that an influential adult might have helped to fill.

My parents urged me to study – to get an education. They wanted me to get a good basis in high school to build upon in university. In high school I didn't really learn much about preparation for entry into work. All the time it was just drilled into my head: "If you don't have an education you won't go anywhere in life." My vice-principal told me that I would be a dishwasher if I dropped out of school – and I was, for about six months.

A co-op program would have helped me face the job market with more knowledge about working conditions and lifestyle. I did eventually learn these things. One thing I now know is that you can go to work and sweat for eight hours and come home sore and tired but if you don't have higher education you won't bring home much money.

Since then I've been to high school, college and university. I'm not stupid. When I was in school I had dreams of great and noble careers. I never found anyone who would nurture these dreams and help me make them concrete. All I heard was "Get an education, get an education." Nobody tried to stop me from getting high or cutting classes or dropping out. I was foolish. I was lured by what I thought was freedom – money, drugs, and alcohol, and doing whatever pleased me at the time. I think that in high school the narrowness of this kind of action should be exposed.

Conservative   Another youth takes careers seriously, though not very imaginatively. She is a career conservative.

I'm debating between staying at my present job or going back to school. For many years a diploma wasn't important; getting loads of experience was my goal. Although it's true you do need experience, it seems now that I'm married and have a daughter, a diploma comes into play. I feel I missed out on something by never accomplishing Grade Twelve.

Experience is what got me positions so far. I'm secretary to the executive director. For some that would be the extent of their goals, but not for me. I don't wish to stay at this level forever. I want to accomplish more, knowing I'm capable of doing so.

Employers more and more want to know what you've achieved. They want to know if you have a diploma, what your average was and how long you were at your jobs. Don't give up, take one realistic step at a time. If you're in school, get experience through co-op or a part-time job. This way you get the feel of work and it also gives you a chance to change your mind about future goals. School is where your future lies; if you leave it too soon or don't get all you can from it, it will turn out to your disadvantage.

Innovative   Another youth is an imaginative risk taker, an innovator venturing into a field that permits expression of values and requires further education and training.

The "basics" (three Rs) come from school and values come from home. I was lucky enough to have a family that supported my own decisions about my future.

Secondary school preparation is different for various people. There are those students "pegged" to go on to university, and those that aren't. That's fine as long as students know what they want but that's hard in secondary school! Kids are often led down the wrong path. My old high school is presently a vocational high school and allows students practical experience and the chance to use what they're learning. I think that's great – especially for people who need to see the value in an education and how it can be useful (i.e., getting a job).

I work at a centre for the handicapped. Preparation for social service work comes from home, school, friends, and experiences. These lead you to have the patient, positive, and caring attitude that is needed. Of course, reading, writing, and arithmetic are essential.

But what school really shows is that you are trainable. The right state of mind and interest in this type of work is not something that you can learn through education alone. Knowledge of the field and people comes from school and the community.

I took a Man-in-Society class in Grade Thirteen that touched on social problems and special populations and I loved it. Maybe that was what sparked some interest, but for as long as I can remember I have enjoyed working with people. I loved high school, and so far I really like my job.

CHAPTER THREE

The Family's Heritage:
Class, Gender, and Ethnicity

Home, school and work are different worlds. Students are expected to be so dependent. Then all of a sudden, they're out there on their own. If they don't have a supportive family to fall back on, as I had, they're really lost.

Male, skilled worker, 24.

When I was 15, I started doing drugs intensely. My parents and I moved into a new house. I couldn't live up to their goals for me. Had my first serious relationship with a man 27 years old. Which matured me faster in certain ways than other ways. Went back and got my diploma by the age of 19 and moved away from home and in with my boyfriend for two and a half years. During this time, I started working full time as a nanny.

Female, unskilled worker, 24.

The young adults quoted here had a typically stressful launching into the working world. Both talk about the influence of the family, but their relations at home were utterly different. One speaks gratefully of his parents' support. The other, alienated at home, wandered in an episodic journey into underemployment and dependence.

Socialization into maturity is usually marked by tension between individual wishes and powerful social structures such as family, school, and work. On one hand, individual choices, on the other, social pressure. The tension is most intense and fateful during adolescence. As the model in chapter 1 suggests, the struggle occurs not only in the climates of family, school, and workplace; it is intensified by the invidious distinctions of class, gender, and ethnicity. As this chapter will show, family background points youth in directions that are later refined in school and early work experiences. By then, directions have become rutted channels for many, especially those from disadvantaged homes (Woelfel and Haller 1971; D.L. Thomas 1974).

SOCIAL CLASS, GENDER, ATTAINMENT, AND NORMS

Class is the most persistent structural determinant of youth's goals and attainment. It operates through the educational and occupational levels of parents, with all that these entail – understanding, prestige, income, lifestyle, and social skills. Canadian studies for several decades have used "social reproduction" models to explain the intergenerational transmission of class (Hall and McFarlane 1962; Breton et al. 1972; Porter et al. 1982; Anisef et al. 1982; Krahn and Lowe 1991; Crysdale 1980; Crysdale and MacKay 1980, 1994; Axelrod and Anisef 1995). Findings consistently show a positive relation between one generation's status and that achieved by the next. It is typical of industrialized nations that children who are multiply deprived perform less well than others at school and in the labour force (Faure 1972; Ashton and Lowe 1991). These patterns are reproduced as each generation is socialized into structures that perpetuate values, beliefs, attitudes, skills, and practices (Althusser 1969; Bourdieu and Passeron 1977; Bowles and Gintis 1976; Heinz 1996). This works to the advantage of children when parents foster positive consonance in cultural, ideological and economic identity. But dissonance, or negative consonance, leads to the perpetuation of disadvantage (see chapter 7).

Three subtheories are often proposed to explain class reproduction. *Cultural deficit theory* attributes the failure of lower-class children to the relative absence of an environment that helps develop intelligence. *Cultural difference theory* rejects the portrayal of lower-class cultures as inferior, suggesting that many schools are white, male, middle-class environments that are at odds with the values, attitudes, linguistic codes, and communication systems provided by peers and families (D.L. Thomas 1974; Bernstein

1977; Bourdieu and Passeron 1977). *Cultural reproduction theory* emphasizes the ways the family mediates between children's class origin and the school as the critical source of inequality. Schools tend to classify children according to family background, age, sex, and race, by means of curricula, pedagogical principles, spatial organization, and evaluation criteria. Often students are downgraded on the basis of cultural hurdles rather than improvement and potential.

The place of class in educational aspiration is shown in Table A–4 where there are moderate correlations between parents' educational and occupational levels on one hand, and their aspirations for their children's education on the other. This perception by youth of parental encouragement spills over into their feelings about what teachers and employers expect of them in terms of education. Strong coefficients show that parental class also affects the educational level actually attained.

Conditions for school attainment are specified by average marks and effort (see Table 2–3). Parents' class, especially mothers' occupation, affected marks directly. Children of higher-status parents won better marks than others, sometimes without more effort.

The advantage of status is carried forward into youth's present job levels and their expectations for ten years ahead (Table A–5). Mother's status carries more weight than father's. Ethnicity and gender do not make much difference in expectations, but women get lower-level jobs. High expectations generally lead to better jobs. But being a woman and starting at an inferior level compound the likelihood of lower-level employment.

The observation in earlier sections that girls surpass boys in educational attainment is specified in Table A–6. Girls tended more than boys to score between 70 and 79 percent on tests, exams, and assignments; the same proportion of both genders won marks over 80 percent. Boys more than girls tended to drop out without a diploma. Girls were a little more likely to go on to post-secondary education, both in college and university.

Table A–7 shows that the present job levels of our sample youth were not significantly different by gender, but men were paid much more, with a mean of $589 per month, compared with $367 for women. Men also received more on-the-job training, though the mean level for both was less than one week. Young women were encouraged to do well at school and to plan for good jobs but at work they faced structured barriers. Most were clustered into traditionally female ghettos.

To measure gender norms and observe differences between the principal players in transition, we constructed a scale based on five questions. The questions and results appear in Tables 3–1 and 3–2.

Scores for the five gender norms were added to obtain total scores. Those who based answers on gender were ranked low (1), and those who refused to put conditions on equality were ranked high (3). In between, the largest proportion of all players would favour one or the other gender, depending chiefly on perceived ability (2). Overall, employers ranked highest in equalitarian norms, followed closely by youth, parents and, finally, teachers. The broad tendency was towards equality and flexibility.

Why, then, are young women so disadvantaged in employment? One explanation is that while equalitarianism has come to be seen widely as just, *discriminatory structures and practices* are so engrained that they obstruct equality. Comments by some women and men belie the norms that the majority feel constrained to approve publicly. This is an issue of power and money, but deeper still lie the apparitions of prejudice and fear, the heritage of centuries of oppression. Like other deeply lodged values, gender prejudice is nursed in many families, hidden in some school practices, and often countenanced at work (D.L. Thomas 1974).

Strikingly, the overall scores of gender-equality norms held by young men and women are not statistically different. But outward conformity with flexible norms, even among young adults, may conceal lurking, internalized prejudice. Equalitarianism in theory does not vary widely by social class or ethnicity. It is held somewhat more strongly by youth with higher education, who had more say in the family about their transition to the workplace and who have higher job expectations.

Qualitative data illustrate the quasi-egalitarian nature of the normative stance of both men and women in the study. Often traditional roles have given way, not to complete sharing, but to neotraditional roles. Both a husband and wife may work, but the husband's work usually comes first in terms of the amount earned, family influence, and location of family residence. Most wives may work only if they are capable of holding two jobs, one outside and the other inside the home (Mandell 1987, 177).

Table 3–1
Sex Role Norms, according to Youth and Parents (Percentages)

	Parents			Youth		
	1 One Gender	2 Conditional Equality	3 Both, Unconditionally	1 One Gender	2 Conditional Equality	3 Both, Unconditionally
1 With limited funds in a family, which youth should continue past high school?	7	72	21	6	84	11
2 Is a career more important in a family for a man or woman?	15	44	41	18	56	26
3 If both spouses are working, who is responsible for household chores and child care?	3	97		3	97	
4 Are some courses usually more difficult for students of one gender?*	19	30	51	12	27	61
5 Who make the best employers: men or women?	31	70		27	61	12
Composite Gender Equality Scale†	Low 29	Middle 56	High 15	Low 23	Middle 60	High 18

* As replies to this question did not fit set categories, we recorded values disclosed by responses as follows:
1 = by innate nature, 2 = by actual practice, 3 = neither by nature nor practice.
† Total scores of 10 or under = low, 11–12 = middle, 13–15 = high.

Table 3–2
Sex Role Norms, according to Teachers and Employers (Percentages)

	Teachers			Employers		
	1 One Gender	*2* Conditional Equality	*3* Both, Unconditionally	*1* One Gender	*2* Conditional Equality	*3* Both, Unconditionally
1 With limited funds in a family, which youth should continue past high school?	4	96		6	83	12
2 Is a career more important in a family for a man or woman?	6	92	3	22	43	35
3 If both spouses are working, who is responsible for household chores and child care?	1	99		6	95	
4 Are some courses usually more difficult for students of one gender?*	8	15	77	10	31	59
5 Who make the best employers: men or women?	3	97		24	66	11
Composite Gender Equality Scale†	Low	Middle	High	Low	Middle	High
	28	66	7	22	58	20

* We recorded values for question 4 to fit replies, as follows:

1 = by innate nature, 2 = by actual practice, 3 = neither by nature nor practice.

† Total scores of under 10 = low, 11–12 = middle, 13–14 = high.

Women are still held to be primarily responsible for housework, childcare, emotional nurturing, and household management. The reasons for this include women's continued economic dependence on men and traditional socialization. Many youth still think of gender with the more conventional division of tasks, stating, for example, that "females care more about families," or, "You need a mother at home to have a family." One perceptive young adult commented, "Women must have steady jobs and daycare to enable them to participate in careers equally with men."

Despite ideological emphasis on the desirability of egalitarian marital relationships, Canadian women generally do not share power, decision making, or workloads equally with their male partners. Rather, they engage in double days that are often full of angst and stress brought on by sexist behaviour, demands and values (Duffy et al. 1989). A study of Nova Scotian households, for example, disclosed that on average men do one hour of housework a day while women do two and a half hours, regardless of whether they also work outside the home (Day 1990, 36; Armstrong and Armstrong 1994).

In light of these facts, youth's expectations of shared domestic labour seem unrealistic. Some parents note that domestic labour is rarely shared, stating, for example, that "most females do more than half the housework." More bluntly, "the reality is, females do the household work."

Youth sometimes reflected sexist childrearing:

My father is a chauvinist. He never encouraged me in school. He felt he wasn't a man because he didn't have a son.

My mother wanted me to complete college. Dad didn't really care which way as long as I had a job.

The son is more likely to be the breadwinner so he should go to university – if something were to happen to him, the daughter could marry.

A minority of parents took explicitly sexist positions regarding academic futures and abilities:

Only sons should go to university ...

Females and math don't go together ...

Training females who leave during pregnancy makes it difficult for employers.

It appears that males and females experience different family realities that shape their educational and occupational aspirations and attainments. Males are more likely to be encouraged to pursue professional careers, unencumbered by domestic duties, and to experience democratic decision making within the family (see chapter 7). People who grow up thinking that their beliefs count, their ideals are efficacious, and their views considered are likely to be self-confident (cf. Porter et al. 1982, 133).

Decision making and efficacy are traditionally associated with masculinity, power, and control. Young men from all classes and ethnic groups grow up expecting that their opinions, demands, and needs will take precedence over those of females. For women family socialization patterns reinforce ethics of caring, passive nurturing, and submission. They are rewarded for fitting in, being compliant, responsible, and mindful of others. In contrast, young men are socialized into patterns of active dominance, control, manipulation, emotional inexpressiveness, assertiveness, self-centred planning and execution of goals. Men define the norms that women subscribe to. Women plan futures involving others: men dream of solo accomplishments.[1]

Jean Anyon (1983, 19–37) suggests that gender development occurs differently for men and women. For girls it involves attempts to cope with and resolve contradictory social messages regarding what they should do and be. For them the ideology of femininity – domestic nurturing, submissiveness, and noncompetitiveness – contradicts the ideology of public success.[2]

Influential Others

Canadian research on educational attainment has documented the primary role of parents in helping children establish educational aspirations and accomplish their goals (Porter et al. 1982, 149, etc). Ways of doing this include helping with schoolwork and career planning. Discussion in the previous chapter shows that parents are the most important "others" in guiding youth through transition. Peers are next, followed by spouses, then teachers, and, trailing the others, employers.

The persistence of class background as a predictor of youth's prospects in the labour market is shown in Table A–8. The educational attainment of parents has a significant impact on their children's job expectations and anticipated work satisfaction.

Maternal occupation also has a positive effect on pay, training, future intrinsic satisfaction, and, in particular, job expectation. Paternal occupation affects the last two outcomes but not the first two. (The reasons for these effects are discussed in chapter 8.)

Other correlates of help by parents are documented (Table A–4). Help from mothers, in particular, raises youth's efforts at school. Self-help correlates slightly with mothers' occupations. Job aspirations are raised consistently by parental hopes, and strongly when the hopes are shared by both parents. Marks at secondary school benefit only slightly from parental status.

The educational attainment of youth and prospects of reaching higher-level jobs rise markedly when both parents convey high hopes. The correlations are positive, direct, and strong between youth's self-help and years of education, effort at school, expectations, marks in the last year of high school, and current job (not shown).

Parents tend to minimize their own helpfulness. One-third of parents said that the family had very little influence and only 23 percent said their influence had been strong. Yet, asked to rank the help they receive, youth with higher educational and occupational achievements rank parental help as notably strong and consistent.

Carol Smart (1990) characterizes parental involvement with children as gender stereotyped. Fathers "care about" their children's well-being while mothers "care for" their offspring. The former entails verbal encouragement and articulation of aspirations while the latter involves the day-to-day work of monitoring homework, dealing with teachers, assessing success and failure. Help with schooling is part of child care and domestic labour, a task traditionally performed almost exclusively by mothers. It is thus not surprising that youth acknowledge their mothers' advice and support as the leading external help in transition.

Another probable reason for the greater influence of mothers is that, in comparison with fathers, many were deprived of the education and occupations they had hoped for in their own youth. Fathers are twice as likely to be supervisors, managers, or professionals, and more fathers enjoy intrinsic job satisfaction. To compensate for their disappointing subordination, many mothers pass on ambition to their children.

Over half of the parents in our study said they discussed education with their children about once a month. Mothers, especially of the middle class, were more likely than others to attempt to influence their children's progress.

THE SCHOOL AND CLASS, GENDER, AND ETHNICITY

Family-school-work relationships, tempered by class, gender and ethnic differences, are ambiguous, uneven, tense, sometimes complementary but often conflictual. Schools have been assigned contradictory responsibilities – reproducing a workforce already segmented along the lines of class, gender and ethnicity while simultaneously developing social mobility, equality and human rights.[2]

Some critics observe that corporate executives regard the school as an institution for legitimating business and for encouraging students to accept its mores while lowering expectations and demands of the system (Livingstone 1985: 76). Schools see themselves as engaging students in learning social, moral and life skills that go beyond business agendas. Schools are "active cultural spheres" (Giroux 1981), sometimes both sustaining and resisting economic values and beliefs.

Vocational education, which until recently provided most students for co-op programs, represents the school's compromise between the contradictory demands of society (Clarke and Willis 1988). The vocational/academic split suggests that there are at least two transitional channels, each further complicated by class, gender, and ethnicity.

A rational model of transition would provide that the school should have a major role in guiding young entrants into the labour force (Rist 1986). This picture, however, overstates the present role of schools, especially for high-risk young people, as a positive shaper of employment decisions. It overlooks the attachments that young people form with influential adults and peers, more often outside the school than inside. For about half of youth in North America passage to work is largely haphazard (see chapter 9). For a small minority, passage is being improved by employment-linked programs such as work study and co-operative education[3] (see chapter 5).

Schools reflect the sex and class of their students through curriculum, spatial organization, and evaluation criteria. Critics say that beneath mainline school culture lies an implicit preference for "high culture," stressing complex communication codes, written styles, and verbal articulation based on white male middle-class norms. Students without this "cultural capital" are sometimes thought to lack adequate knowledge and to be out of sync with the school ethos.

Class and gender differences in school performance, as mentioned earlier, appear in average marks during the last year and in the amount of effort students report investing in school work (Table 2–1).

In 1962 Hall and McFarlane reported gender distinction, as did an earlier report on Ontario Grade Thirteen students (Fleming 1957). Porter, Porter, and Blishen (1982) found that girls won better grades than boys. In our study, as we have said, girls got slightly better marks, went slightly further, studied harder, and were more likely to think their teachers wanted them to continue.

Women in higher-than-average-level employment enjoy enhanced prestige and confidence and this is not lost on children. Many mothers, however, work at dull, demeaning, and low-paying jobs and this does not improve their children's prospects. Yet without a second family income youth's chances would be restricted. They and their mothers are in a double bind. Low achievement and underparticipation by poor children begin early and accelerate in later grades.

Who did parents blame when their children did not do well? Not teachers or peers, who are cited by only nine and 12 percent of parents. A child's lack of ambition was cited by 27 percent, "other" people by 22 percent, and "no one" by 31 percent. Only one parent blamed the family. Probably "others" and "no one" were selected by parents who could not decide or who blamed circumstances beyond their control such as divorce, illness, poverty, and alienation.

Many youth and parents, like those in other countries (Weiss 1990; Connell et al. 1982), are critical of schools for not facilitating upward mobility. Although individual teachers are often extolled, youth and parents complain that schools do not adequately prepare children for college *or* non-manual labour. Since the mid-1980s, when our sample left high school, complaints have continued.

Not surprisingly, teachers view the problem differently, holding some parents responsible for a lack of commitment to education. Parents often cannot or will not take part in school functions or monitor their children's education.

Schools, colleges, and universities, usually unwittingly, may condition students through both official and hidden curricula. Official curricula deal with teachers' selection of subjects to be taught, general activities, and official positions within schools. The hidden curricula include varying gender-role messages in textbooks, teachers' interactions and prohibitions, and informal staff hierarchies.

Some youth report blatant sexism:

In one course the teacher was very discriminatory.

Male-oriented novels are used like *The Right Stuff*, with no effort to encourage females. All the material was very "wasp" ...

When I start teaching, I'll encourage women to become scientists and engineers. Gender bias in education is a problem that must be recognized.

Many young women concluded from teachers' attitudes and comments that their careers should lie in health care, education, or social work. But middle-class girls, in particular, think that women should achieve academically in order to improve career prospects. They have relatively high educational and career aspirations. The education of working-class girls is often oriented towards future domestic roles rather than paid labour. By regarding marital and maternal roles as primary, many working-class women treat work as necessary but peripheral and secondary. Their focus on domestic life for personal fulfilment ensures the continued existence of a cheap female labour force (MacDonald 1980; Gaskell 1977).

There is little evidence in Canadian schools of explicit discrimination against minorities; it is not systemic in screening, instruction, or grading. We have seen, however, that some Asians and Orientals perform better than others, followed by those of minority European origin (cf. Isajiw et al. 1993). Our study shows positive correlations between minority origin as a whole and job expectations, innovativeness and elders' consonance in hopes for education. Their advantage over dominant whites is small but consistent.

However, students of Afric-ethno cultures achieve at lower levels and face higher transitional barriers than others. There is no credible evidence that they are less intelligent or able. As with women and those of disadvantaged background, blacks commonly come out short in the distribution of power and its rewards in Western societies. Because few blacks showed up in our sample, we cannot contribute statistically to discussion of possible causes. But qualitative observations confirm their disadvantage in transition.

A cue for understanding the transitional disadvantages faced by black students is provided by an American study showing that in spite of similarities in formal means – courses, marks, and educational level – blacks were often excluded from the personal networks that opened job channels for whites (Royster 1997).

When blacks in Canada were fewer the issue was not widely recognized. But now, because of immigration policies, large numbers of blacks and other visible minorities – Chinese, Korean, Taiwanese, East Indian, Pakistani – are evident in Canadian cities, notably Toronto and Vancouver. Schools bear a heavy burden in recognizing and dealing with racism. Because it is so complex and threatening, many educators don't deal openly with the reality – and promise – of differentness. With little leadership from influential others such as parents, employers, and teachers, minority youth are sometimes confused, fearful, and angry. That's when open conflict may explode in fights and crime. For these youth, education and transition seem to hold little promise.

But others take a different course. When an interviewer asked a group of youth in a black ghetto in Halifax why they thought things should be different, several shot back, "Because God cares for us all equally" (Crysdale 1966).

George J. Sefa Dei, among other social scientists and educators, has analyzed sources of racism and advocates measures to counter it. In *Antiracism Education Theory and Practice* (1996, 135), Dei calls on educators to double their efforts to make excellence accessible to all students. The economic and social cost of not doing so is enormous. "Different" should not mean the same as "unequal" or "incapable." Educators and students need to unlearn stereotypes and build communities of difference with a positive emphasis. Families and employers must be helped to go the same route. We can all live and help create a "culturally, economically and politically democratic society."

To meet this need some boards of education require courses in ethnic studies. Because of the city's large minority populations, the Toronto board is a leader. Within its curriculum division, a centre for equity education offers teacher training for inclusive practice. Since most textbooks now in use were published before differentness received much attention, the centre makes available new materials on inclusive teaching. Over 40 programs are in place. Some include gender and age in addition to differentness arising from ethnicity and race.

CHAPTER FOUR

Education and Transition:
The Salience of Learning

The critical role of education in transition is underlined by its impact on young people's success in finding full-time jobs. In 1992 64 percent of Canadians who had taken programs in 1990 in trades or semi-skilled occupations were employed full time. This compared with 87 percent of those with doctoral degrees. In between employment rose with the level of education. The pattern was similar in 1984 for 1982 graduates and in 1986 for 1984 graduates.

"For 1990 graduates employed full time in 1992, median earnings rose by education level. Doctoral graduates led the way, earning $46,000, followed by master's recipients ($44,000) and bachelor's graduates ($32,000). Career/technician graduates earned $26,000, while trade/vocational graduates made $23,000 ... Median earnings of graduates working full time have remained relatively stable between 1984 and 1992 ... Unemployment among young people fell with higher educational attainment, from a national rate of 20 percent in 1990 for trade/vocational workers to 11 percent for technicians and university graduates (Don Little, referring to Statistics Canada's annual "Canadian Graduates Survey" 1995).

The nexus between education and employment is complicated by the need for large numbers of young adults to blend the two, resulting in more part-time schooling and part-time jobs. Many cannot afford to spend more years full time at school without an income. Moreover, with the shift from the old to the new technological economy, many employers need the flexibility of part-time temporary workers to adapt to change.

With the growth of information technology, education has become more important than ever for employment and youth's place in it. The world market, as discussed in chapter 1, pays a large premium for higher numeracy and literacy skills. In Canada, 7.6 percent of the gross national product is devoted to public education, one of the highest rates in the world.[1] The conviction is spreading, however, that educators and employers must do more together to prepare entrants for jobs in the new economy (Ontario Premier's Council 1990; Ontario, Ministry of Education and Training 1996; OECD 1996A, B; Marquardt 1996, 40–3).

Labour market demand for higher literacy has mounted so rapidly that education has fallen behind. This helps to explain the high dropout rate and stubborn unemployment among those under 25. The relationship between literacy and attainment is reciprocal, each leading to the other.

Basic changes in high school curricula are proposed by the Ontario Ministry of Education and Training in the document *Secondary School Reform Consultation* (1996). Reforms will build on new emphases in elementary grades on self-directed learning, human relations, and career development. In Grades Seven to Ten there will be job observation, shadowing, simulation, and mentoring. In Grades Eleven and Twelve there will be substantive work experience, with a majority of hours in credit courses at job sites under school/employer oversight. While counsellors will urge students to adopt the program, the decision will rest with them after consultation with parents, teachers, and employers. The main instrument for transition will be cooperative education in the upper grades. There will also be more emphasis on mathematics, science, and technology. Saskatchewan, Alberta, British Columbia, Nova Scotia, Newfoundland, and other provinces are moving in similar directions. This is in line with recommendations of the OECD (1996).

But top-down reforms in education do not fare well all over the world. Unless there is purposive participation by teachers, parents, employers, and community groups, little will change. This is concluded by Andy Hargreaves and Michael Fullan in *What's Worth Fighting for Out There?* (1998) Meaningful reform happens only when there are good early childhood programs and interactive infrastructures between teachers' unions, parents, employers, and community bodies. These are common in Sweden but even there reform often breaks down due to failures in communication (cf. chapter 9). Success requires constant vigilance.

In this chapter we compare the attainments of youth with those of their parents and then weigh the roles of parents and teachers in transition. We consider the views of youth, parents, and teachers on the main purpose of education. Finally, we present teachers' suggestions on what might help participants with transition.

PARENTS' AND YOUTH'S EDUCATION – A PERSISTENT GULF BY CLASS AND GENDER

Among sample members there has been an intergenerational decrease in the proportion who left school without a secondary diploma, from 38 percent of fathers and 33 percent of mothers to 30 percent of youth. This was the rate in the mid-1980s when the sample finished high school (Table 4–1). It has fallen since to just below 20 percent where it has lodged.

There has also been a large increase in the proportion who have post-secondary education, 51 percent of the weighted sample (23 percent at college plus 28 percent at university), as against 29 percent of fathers and 31 percent of mothers. This compares with about 38 percent of all Canadians of similar age (OECD 1996). Remember that our sample does not represent the whole population; it is purposive, a cut above average.

While there has been an improvement in the openness of education, attainment continues to be skewed by social class. Status reproduction however, operates for the most part indirectly through students' own values and performance. The two strongest direct predictors of educational level are individual – average marks in the last high school year and job goals (Table A–9).

Some youth disappoint their elders while others from less-advantaged homes move ahead, nourished by ambition and encouragement. As youth approach the end of high school and entrance into the workforce, parents' proximity, personal support, and knowledge of work put them ahead of others in helpfulness (cf. Crysdale and MacKay 1994).

Table 4–1
Level of Education of Sample Youth and Parents (Percentages)

	Youth		Fathers	Mothers
No high school diploma	14	(30*)	38	33
Grade Twelve, Thirteen, incomplete, non-university post-secondary	23	(19)	33	36
Post-secondary, non-university	29	(23)	10	18
University, some, graduated, continuing	34	(28)	19	13
Total %	100	(100)	100	100
	(323)		(301)	(301)

* Numbers are weighted to allow for the actual dropout rate in the Canadian population in the year our sample left high school, 1984–85. Weighting is also warranted because of the higher-than-average status of the sample compared with the population as a whole.

The influence of educators is more complex than that of parents; it is specialized, formal, and secondary. Yet teachers have unmatched control over learning and grading. They are both mentors and judges and, in these somewhat conflicting roles, are expected to apply objective standards and establish good relations with students.

Many teachers build supportive links, as appreciative comments by students show. This happens not only in the classroom; some interact with students after school in sports, the arts, and other activities. Today, however, free time is limited for most students since they may spend as many hours at part-time jobs as at school.

One-third of students do not feel at home in huge schools. They resist authoritarian, impersonal socialization into values and knowledge and can't wait to leave. Paradoxically, most of the sample, having left school five years before, now recognize its crucial place in their fortunes.

THE MAIN PURPOSE OF EDUCATION

The effectiveness of education is viewed differently by actors partly as a result of how they think about its goals. We asked youth, parents, and teachers what the main purpose of education should be. We then asked youth to indicate what, in fact, they thought received greatest emphasis at school.

The results appear in Table 4–2. Almost half of the youth and parents in our sample think that education should first impart social and applied skills, compared with fewer than one-third of teachers. Far more of the latter, over one-half, place at the top the cultivation of the person. Youth and parents place personal growth second.

More than half of the youth say that teachers overemphasize university as the chief goal or stress covering the curriculum and following routine. Youth's views on the purpose of education do not vary with ethnicity. But girls are slightly less pragmatic than boys. The following comments are typical of responses by youth at different levels and stages of transition.

Young professionals and managers   "Education is to pass on knowledge, teach responsibility and prepare for careers," said an oriental Canadian girl who was still at university, preparing for hospital management. "My parents told me to study hard when we came to this country, as we are considered to be inferior to whites. However, I now speak without an accent and have not experienced discrimination. My parents told me not to cause trouble if possible. I've learned that sometimes I have to defend my position."

"The main purpose," another girl said, "should be to learn to think and work. This doesn't end at three o'clock." This girl's parents came from southern Europe; her father is a carpenter and her mother, formerly a nurse, is now a factory worker. In co-op education, the daughter was assigned to an advertising agency. This motivated her to continue to college and she is now a media buyer, negotiating contracts with TV and radio companies.

"The main purposes of education are to expose students to general knowledge and offer guidance for working and living." This young man's parents are from northern Europe. His father is a freight agent and his mother a secretary; neither went past high school. He himself went to college and is a commercial co-pilot.

"Discover how to learn; you'll be doing it all your life. Develop maturity and prepare for the next level." This speaker's parents completed Grade Twelve and are both middle managers. He was placed with an electronics firm through co-op; they asked him to stay on. He took an engineering degree and is testing designs.

Table 4–2
Purpose of Education and Emphasis in Secondary School (Percentages)

	Youth	Parents	Teachers
PURPOSE OF EDUCATION			
Teach social and applied skills	48	47	29
Cultivate the complete person	28	33	51
Transmit values and knowledge	6	9	11
Other main purpose	17	11	9
Totals	99	100	100
Frequencies	(306)	(112)	(232)
MAIN EMPHASIS IN SECONDARY SCHOOL			
Teach social and applied skills	25		
Cultivate the person	11		
Transmit culture	12		
Other main purpose, e.g. covering the curriculum, maintaining routine, etc.	52		
Total	100		
Frequencies	(295)		

Another replied, "The main goal of education should be to teach facts, provide basic moral standards, motivate students to succeed, make learning fun, help students with emotional problems. Not everyone comes from a happy home. If you just drill the three Rs without motivating them, you're wasting time." Her parents didn't get beyond Grade Eight and both have semi-skilled jobs. But they gave her more than material support. She has a university degree and is working as a clerk before resuming studies in medicine.

"Education's chief goal is to transmit culture and values, along with useful skills," said a young engineer whose origins are German and English. He was offered a scholarship to specialize. He took co-op, which helped him decide on a career. His parents didn't go to high school. Like others with similar promise, his beliefs strongly affect his studies and work.

"A good education should help you set your life goals, start you off with skills and give you a well-rounded view of the world." This girl's early goal was teaching but she switched to engineering in university. That's her father's profession. She credits her mother more than her father for encouraging her.

These high achievers are somewhat critical of high school. One said that because of emphasis on competition, many students become aware of inabilities rather than possibilities. He feels there is little to motivate the majority. Another said that schools place more stress on memorizing details than on developing a broad sweep of knowledge. Again, the actual dominant aim was said to be learning to follow instructions, obey rules, and conform to set patterns.

An accountant was more positive: "School helps the weak and encourages the strong." A young entrepreneur said that "school gives a passport to a job but doesn't develop interest or goals." A female engineer said, "Schools prepare you for a job or college, not both."

Returnees   Over one-third of youth said that they planned to return to school within a year, another 22 percent said "possibly," while 43 percent had no such plans. Returnees have mixed feelings about both the ideal and actual purposes of education.

A man who quit in Grade Eleven and plans to go back to finish an apprenticeship said that school gets you ready for the real world, being told what to do, to be responsible. "If you don't get things done, you get a detention. At work you get fired. School offers you the resources and the rest is up to you. One teacher told us slackers, 'I get my pay cheque; you don't.'"

Another young man, in applied engineering, is taking college courses to get an advanced certificate. His parents are both professionals. "Education should be general until upper secondary school, then specialized. It now streams students at too early a stage." This is also the view of a commerce graduate who plans to enter law school. His mother is a professional. His first choice had been medicine, but halfway through the first year he discovered you can't be a doctor if you're colour blind. It would have helped if counsellors had advised him of this.

A different position is taken by a student who lost interest in high school and dropped out to take menial jobs, to the great disappointment of his parents, both teachers. It took several years for him to decide to become a teacher, too, and he is taking evening courses to that end. "By mid-high school," he says, "everyone should be helped to explore job goals, as well as to acquire general knowledge. At present, large numbers of high school students have no goals; earning credits without them is meaningless."

Mid-level careerists   A promotional consultant with a good salary is taking courses to gain perspective in his private as well as occupational life. The main purpose of education is to improve oneself and get ahead. "High school showed me that if you don't apply yourself, you'll be left behind. It's highly competitive and private. I missed a lot because I felt lost in the crowd and lacked the maturity and motivation to take advantage of opportunities."

A few have a wider grasp of the functions of education. A musician who had to struggle with parents and teachers to win freedom writes: "Education is chiefly a method of socialization, to teach values and to integrate the population. While there is specialization in subject and method there is little integration for the person."

Skilled workers   A minority of young workers have improved their skills through apprenticeships and other training programs. An auto mechanic devoted to his work has done it the hard way. At first he didn't get a diploma because he worked up to 40 hours a week while still a student. But he stuck with his goal. With the help of parents and friends, he finally took the college credits he needed and is now a skilled tradesman. "School should adjust to the individual, not the other way around. Trades should have more prestige and kids should all become familiar with different careers. Streaming doesn't do this and limits potential ... just get them through."

A head teller in a bank who has some post-secondary studies is unsure of his long-range goals. Partly because of a separated family, he had little guidance and felt lost during high school. He said education, above all, should develop a person through general knowledge and career guidance. He didn't get the latter and drifted through a series of unrelated jobs.

One girl didn't complete high school in spite of good grades, partly because she worked long hours during the term. She has a secretarial job. She felt that high school should prepare a person for maturity, including a career. With little guidance at home or at school, she couldn't see how general subjects related to her interests. There was nothing to hold her.

Semi-skilled and unskilled workers   Many youth for various reasons were uncommitted or felt excluded. Most in this situation never got a diploma. Some longed for meaningful jobs but never got on track.

Some have emotional problems. One lad of minority race was so shy that he suffered from attempts to include him in school activities and dropped out. His brother is having a similar experience. The interviewer asked to see their art work, which was extremely good. But somehow their talent was never discovered at school. "Education should help you become a better person, but at school the first goal is to get high marks. I'd still like to learn a skilled trade."

A barkeeper gives his friends credit for trying to help him but admits he is too shy to help himself. He sees no future and is not interested in a career. "School provides opportunities to learn and get established. But they stress attendance and homework. School was scary. Teachers didn't seem to care except to tell you how much education you needed to make it. We were not adult enough to be confident. We needed more counselling personally and about careers. More help for slow learners. More of everything except rules."

Another "dropout" works part time as a shipper for auto parts. It's like a full-time job but without benefits. He worked 40 hours a week while at school. He'd like to be a tradesman but hasn't enough credits. "I haven't found a place yet where I fit in. There should be closer ties between school and work, so students would know what skills are needed. Actually, school is geared to higher education and not to future work." His father had some college education and was manager of a computer firm; his mother had little education and was a factory worker. Both parents tried to help but there was little consonance between their hopes and those of teachers and employers. He didn't take co-op.

The son of professionals, now a cook, used to think that a job was more important than schooling. Now he realizes he was wrong and is disillusioned about himself and society. He went to university, then switched to trade school, though he had good marks. "A counsellor advised me to. The main purpose of education should be to learn responsibility and provide basic knowledge so that students can decide what they need to start a career. This didn't happen for me."

A girl who had no occupational goals left school without a diploma. She works as a nanny but would stop if she could afford it, to care for her family. Education, she says, should teach proper behaviour and basic skills for employment. She thinks it does the former but not the latter. It should also help with life planning. No one helped her in her transition to work. Her parents didn't have much education and she never heard of co-op.

Another girl who left school without a diploma is a part-time cashier at a grocery store. While at school she worked 26 hours a week, which hurt her studies. She was always tired, had no friends and took no part in school activities. She took work-study for two weeks but not co-op. She hates her job and would like to train as a secretary, but this is not likely to happen as she needs an income to care for her child. "Education should help students prepare for work, instead of stressing more education."

The uncommitted Now a secretary with no chance of promotion, one young woman would like to go back to school and improve her position but can't because she's raising a daughter. She completed a computer course at college and earned high marks. She lives with her parents, neither of whom went beyond mid-high school. "Education should have a practical side, teach responsibility and help you deal with people. In school there was too much emphasis on going to university."

A junior clerk is willing to take training for promotion and likes her job but says, "It will never be a career. The minute I leave the office I start enjoying social life. Work is a means to that end." She lives with friends who are her main helpers in facing problems. "High school, where I earned a Grade Twelve diploma, taught me the basics along with job skills. But they emphasized authority, homework, and exams. Other than applied subjects, I hated school with a passion. Teachers didn't make classes interesting; they were happy if you sat quietly. It's serious when so many teachers dislike their jobs and their students. They should have a breather from the classroom and update teaching skills. I know it's a tough job, but so much depends on them doing it well."

A young cabinet maker has a Grade Thirteen diploma but was not interested in school and put minimal effort into his studies. He doesn't want more training and hopes to start his own furniture shop someday. "Education should prepare students for life as adults and help them find work. But high school is geared chiefly to those bound for university and doesn't do much in searching for suitable work. I never heard of co-op."

A junior secretary says she's in a dead-end job but it doesn't bother her too much – family and social life are more important. She will retrain as technologies require but is not anxious for advancement. "Schools should provide real-world knowledge and useful skills. In some ways schools are good symbols of workplaces; if you skip school you are penalized and if you are unreliable at work you won't last."

Young adults understand the power that education exerts on their lives. Some have sufficient independence and ambition to adapt education to their goals. But most simply go with the flow. Almost half of the youth sample, especially those who did not take post-secondary, feel that school can be improved by linking general knowledge with preparation for work.

One key condition for positive adaptation is that someone – parent, peer, teacher, or early employer – should care for youth as people and encourage them to find a creative and gratifying pathway through school and into work.

CORRELATES OF PARENTS' ASPIRATIONS FOR YOUTH

Educational objectives do not stand in isolation from other goals; they are bound firmly to occupational hopes. The correlation coefficient between parental hopes for youth's education and those for jobs is a fairly strong $r = .431$.

Among antecedents of parental aspirations for youth are their own education and jobs, along with the help they give their children in transition. In the minds of youth parental hopes for schooling are associated with teachers' hopes. This suggests that youth themselves act as catalysts in melding the hopes of parents and teachers.

THE VIEWS OF TEACHERS

On Educative Roles

Suggestions were invited from teachers on how to help students in transition. Their ideas combine philosophy, content, and method.

A drama teacher said that the key is the teacher. Curricula, methods, and techniques all flow through that person.

Drama helps transition by developing verbal skills needed in all interaction, including interviewing, negotiating, and operating procedures. Whenever one actor relates to another, roles are created which express values, power is exercised, goods and services are exchanged.

The family has more influence than the rest of the cast. If a parent doesn't care about learning, the student won't either. Employers could help by permitting employees time off to attend school or college part time. Managers might take part in planning education, contributing to shop, classroom learning, and orientation to work.

The main purpose of education is to connect youth to the culture, traditions, and knowledge of their country, not isolate them. This will help prepare them to make decisions that deal with the changing world and their place in it.

Co-op is a useful way to make connection. Everyone can benefit. Start it sooner, in elementary school, so that students in Grades Seven and Eight can begin to consider seriously their future and the steps needed to get there.

Not all teachers would agree with this view of education's main goal. A teacher in the same school thinks that closer ties with employers would have negative results: "School is not meant to replace job training." But the same teacher, a science specialist, thinks that every student could benefit from co-op. It helps students understand different positions with a view to setting goals. Contradictorily, he adds, "The big problem is staffing. Every co-op student is subsidized by larger classes everywhere, to the detriment of all."

A math teacher has given up on parent participation. But she thinks that the three aims of education are to get a job, to think, and to socialize. "Students at all levels should benefit from co-op as everyone has to work today. Students must take co-op to prepare for the shocker of working. No one will write a note to the boss to cure everything, and no more sleeping in. You must produce for the first time in your life. The great advantage of out-of-classroom education is that you have a different powerful adult to answer to."

In the same school, a resource teacher thinks that his subjects help by implanting critical thought, love of reading, and information retrieval – all necessary for independent learning.

More effort should go into the inclusion of parents as youth advance in schooling. While teaching is different from training, employers should share with teachers in orienting students to develop background for judgments about work and possible occupations.

As a parent I want schools to concentrate on developing in my children the ability to think creatively and systematically. For example, closer ties between home, school, and work could be achieved by internship, in which students follow and assist specialists on the job. This would mean sharing resources, staff, technology, and money.

The main purpose of education? Learning how to make intelligent evaluations, acquiring the art of living, stimulating independent lifetime learning. Getting a job follows.

On Dialoguing with Parents

Most teachers agree that without parental support students are at a serious disadvantage. Some have suggestions for improving relations with them.

More frequent and informal reports on student performance, combined with invitations to attend seminars on how parents might help ... Newsletters to the community, with anecdotes, examples, puzzles, true and false, announcements of career days, exhibitions, visits to workplaces, return coupons with questions, comments ... Informal and attractive outlines of courses, with descriptions, purposes, notes from employers on what they expect of part-time workers, typical career planning, especially towards the end of semesters or terms, as aids in course selection for the next session ... Cues to parents on how to learn along with their adolescents, in partnership; how to deal together with important issues such as differences, quarrels, racial and ethnic tensions, dating, health (physical and mental), values, and beliefs.

As many parents cannot attend school events because of job schedules, care of small children, and shyness, school committees might recruit them to share in planning community/school events on their own turf. This might be an ethnic association, group of churches, local recreation centre, even an apartment common room. Size is not important ... Boards of Trade and similar groups could be approached to share with parents in planning "Meet Your Teachers" events, when current topics might be dealt with in discussion groups on home study, with help from parents, popular TV shows, with implications for goals, lifestyle, learning, and interpersonal relations ... the benefits and burdens of part-time work, co-op education.

At the least, bulletins should go home on resources at school for counselling on personal and career matters, co-op education, time management, study cues. Bulletins might have tear-offs for questions and comments, to be returned to the school ... In local news weeklies inform parents of schools' offerings; use an informal, narrative style. Have a question/answer column ... Cooperate with an intermediate school in planning a school fun fair in the autumn, with booths for food, games, advice on courses, studies, careers ... Provide handouts.

As most teenagers will become parents, high schools should offer courses in life management [such courses are required in Alberta] that deal with social relations, dating, work-study, career search, health, and parenting. Many schools have advisory councils, including area health, employment, recreation, religious and civic leaders, and parents. Some councils are attached to co-op programs.

On Relations with Employers

Teachers' suggestions on this subject fall into two types: school-centred and workplace-centred projects. Some ventures are both. The most common suggestion is co-op education. This requires that firms help to plan, monitor and evaluate students in placements. Some firms are active on a regional advisory committee, helping to find placements and to plan curricula. Employers might come to schools to talk about work opportunities and advance planning. Their visits may be structured as panels or seminars in which teachers and parents take part. Employers should be invited to speak at Career Days and arrange plant and office tours. Other suggestions follow.

Twinning, or partnership between firms and schools, is developing. Also mentoring, where professionals and specialists help groups of students conduct experiments or field studies. Hold roundtable discussions at staff meetings, both in schools and workplaces. Groups of companies might offer awards and prizes for achievement in co-op and other subjects. Regional half-day conferences on part-time jobs, in which bosses, teachers, parents, and students participate. These could be reported in the media.

Arrange for student volunteers to help Saturdays in hospitals, seniors' homes, TV and radio studios, factories, and tourist offices.
Training and contracts about obligations and rights would protect
those involved ... Communication with groups of employers on
how youth may prepare for responsible work roles through mutual fostering of responsibility, honesty, and good citizenship.
Schools and firms should offer awards for effort and work relations.

Canvass employers to let schools know precisely what they want
from schools and students in ethics, relationships, communica-
tive, numeric, and technical skills, commitment. Publicize findings in community media. Recruit retired workers, artists and
others with experience in techniques, management and entre-
preneurship to help occasionally or regularly in classes, group
projects, and advisements.

English, drama, and trades classes could cooperate with employers to produce videotapes on learning at jobs. These could be
used to advise students of requirements for occupations. Part-time
apprenticeships, where students can get credit for courses in high
school and be paid part of a journeyman's wages, should be encouraged.

CHAPTER FIVE

Cooperative Education:
A Bridging Program

TOWARDS THE INTEGRATION
OF EDUCATION AND EMPLOYMENT

The problems in youth's entry into the workforce have been widely researched (Anisef et al. 1982; Canada Employment and Immigration Commission 1983; Ontario, Ministry of Education 1988; Ontario, Ministry of Skills Development 1987, 1989; Canadian Education Association 1983; King and Hughes 1985; Gilbert et al. 1993; Conference Board of Canada 1995B; Crysdale and MacKay 1994; Sharpe et al. 1996). Numerous government efforts have addressed this concern. These initiatives, launched when unemployment is high, serve the need for skill development, chiefly among out-of-work youth, as an alternative to insurance or welfare payments.[1] However, once recessions are over, the programs usually lapse. Few longstanding structures integrate work training across education and business lines. Further, as we have found, less than one-quarter of the private sector assume responsibility for sustained training (Canada Employment and Immigration Commission 1983).

In the past few years initiatives by provincial and federal governments have improved the prospects for closer integration among students. These include sponsoring and setting guidelines for cooperative and work education. The programs provide some students with an early understanding of work settings, roles, responsibilities, and career opportunities. The strength of cooperative education lies in the support students receive from schools.

Its weakness lies in dependence on business for supervised placements.

Work education grew slowly from modest beginnings in the 1960s, but with increased government support it has burgeoned in recent years. About 130,000 students now take part in some form of work education. But they comprise only about eight percent of all high school students and 17 percent of those in Grades Eleven and Twelve. The vast majority still have not been reached. Programs to strengthen curricula so as to better prepare students for employment in the information age are being introduced in Ontario, Saskatchewan, British Columbia, Alberta, Nova Scotia, and other provinces.

This chapter describes and evaluates programs in Ontario and Alberta, where they have been most fully developed. We discuss underlying theories and the background and attainments of students who enrol. We compare views of former students, parents, teachers, and employers on program effectiveness. Finally we assess a shorter variation – work-study.

PROGRAMS IN ALBERTA AND ONTARIO

Alberta has three main programs: "work experience" (co-op), where on-the-job practice and class instruction provide training and theory; "work-study," with introductory lessons on work and visits to job sites, usually in middle school; and a Career and Life Management (CALM) program, which has been required of all senior secondary students since 1988. Work experience and CALM courses each earn direct credits.

Work experience courses at different levels provide opportunities for students to explore careers at workplaces; the time spent at each workplace ranges from 75 hours to 250 hours. CALM has a component, Careers and the World of Work, that explores requirements for careers, human relations, and the rights and responsibilities of workers and managers. Work-study is offered for one to four weeks within various credit subjects. It may be taught in junior or senior high school.

Alberta's Education ministry issues detailed expectations for Work Experience and CALM and provides written and visual resource materials. Boards of education and schools specify curricula. Schools stress student interaction and participation, calling for written journals, group work, assignments, exams, major projects, and presentations.

The requirement that all high school students should take the CALM course aids them in thinking of careers. But more is needed for an intimate knowledge of specific jobs, leading to a firm commitment. That need is more fully met in work experience programs.

Work experience offers, for credit, longer courses related to on-site jobs as an integral part of a school program and under the joint supervision of a teacher and employer. The teacher or coordinator selects and approves suitable placements, obtains the consent of students through a contract with school and employers, establishes evaluation criteria, ensures that instructional practice suits the needs of students, and supervises them on-site at least once in every placement. The students are not paid, except in credits, but may be hired outside the course, for example, during holidays. There has been a marked increase in the number of advanced-level students in work experience, along with an expansion of topics.

Up-to-date computer information is also available from a wide variety of materials, including "Choices," which covers almost one thousand careers. Improvements have enhanced transitional counselling and education. In some schools, up to 70 percent of senior students use these resources.

Alberta is increasing the emphasis on career planning and development through curricula and school practice, offering new initiatives over the next few years.

Ontario proposals for the reform of secondary education in preparation for work were covered in chapter 4. The discussion document recommends that all students in upper secondary grades be urged to take at least one credit course in co-op (Ontario, Ministry of Education and Training 1996). Policies regarding cooperative education in Ontario were stated in a Ministry of Education document in 1989 (Ontario, Ministry of Education). Experiments began in the 60s in a few schools and in 1984 cooperative education was regularized as school policy (Crysdale and MacKay 1994). Procedures establish standards, broaden scope, and include pre-employment instructions, selection and supervision of students, placement at work stations, and monitoring.

Registration in Ontario co-op education grew rapidly in the 1980s. The upward curve has flattened slightly, and in 1995 about 66,200 took part, mostly in senior years. About 40 percent were at the advanced level. Short work-study programs are not included in this calculation. Virtually all boards of education in metro areas participate. About 60 percent of registrants are female.

Advanced or university-bound students dominate in science-related courses and match non-university-bound students in English and physical education co-op courses. The largest registration is in business, guidance/life skills, and technical programs.

Highlights of the policy and procedure statement follow

structured pre-course individual interviews;

a guaranteed suitable placements;

required pre-placement orientation of 20 hours, covering self-assessment, job readiness, social skills, health and safety, labour unions, and school and workplace expectations;

at least one structured interview with a prospective supervisor/employer prior to placement;

an individualized training plan to be devised by the second week of placement;

direct monitoring by a teacher at least three times per course;

at least three formal written appraisals by employers, and integration sessions of at least five hours per course;

The setting of course grades by a teacher in consultation with the employer and subject-specific teacher;

in-school components of at least one-third of credit hours for the course and not less than one-half for the placement component for a total of 110 hours; and

coordination of co-op education with whole programs at the school and board levels.

In Ontario and other provinces, training for teachers in co-op education is provided by faculties of Education and in-service workshops by boards. In many schools programs are available in every subject where there is student demand. Advanced students now have wider opportunities for suitable placement.

Community/school partnerships are spreading. Science students in one Peel school are attached to the nature museum in Toronto. In another school there is a partnership with a coal-burning generating station. Students, mostly from science courses, are assigned to technical positions in the station and employees use the school library, gym, and cafeteria (Dransutavicius 1988; Conference Board of Canada 1995c).

Guelph schools have a highly developed co-op program, reaching all secondary schools in Wellington County. The program bridges the public and separate systems and receives enthusiastic support from the Chamber of Commerce and the Labour Council. It's programs include one on exceptional students and another on women in technology. There are satellite campuses at businesses and industries. The ratio of co-op and work-study teachers to students is one to ten, higher than elsewhere in Ontario.

Youth in Ottawa have access to a wide range of placements. Programs are school-based and respond to community needs. Initiatives by teachers are encouraged by principals, who have final authority over curricula and staff allocations. Staff committees review programs and procedures under the supervision of coordinators and in consultation with employers.

One school has programs for students with learning disabilities, gifted students, those interested in law enforcement or physical education, francophones, specialists in medicine, and drama students through the Children's Theatre. Courses may enlist the help of non-school professionals as mentors. One project tested medical kits in the field; the mentor was a biochemist at a hospital clinic.

Another Ottawa school has a concentration in geriatrics, working with a medical facility. A large proportion of advanced students are involved, particularly in medicine, law, accounting, child care, and teaching. The principal selects cooperative education personnel on the basis of commitment since much of their work must be done after 4:00 P.M., then on relationships with others, experience, and, finally, credentials from university programs.

The third Ottawa sample school is in a working-class area that has many new Canadians. Almost half of the students are returnees, mostly in short programs. There is strong emphasis on social skills, self-confidence, and cultural and social enrichment. Work exploration through job shadowing and other means is provided in Grade Nine and Ten, giving students an early start in planning their careers. The principal and staff at this school believe that all students should take co-op education, as do growing numbers of parents and youth. The school is also involved in partnerships with employers.

A strong feature of co-op education and work-experience education in all provinces is voluntary membership in county, provincial, and national associations. The Co-operative Career and Work Education Association of Canada coordinates initiatives and provides liaison between local and provincial units and the federal employment ministry. These associations give form to what has become an educational movement. Voluntary associations, however, lack the power to bring about changes in structure to improve transition for the vast majority of Canadian youth.

THEORY AND ANALYSIS

North American labour market and education policies have developed reactively. Using schools to reproduce society has become suspect because it reinforces distinction by social class. In response, programs tend to be of two kinds. The majority offer a general preparation for post-secondary education while a lesser number are specialized and innovative. The latter have a shorter term. Voucher systems, ungraded content, and holistic orientations characterize these programs.

The global market dynamic is producing two societies – rich and poor – within and beyond national boundaries. Today the classical model of free, market-driven supply and demand is not likely both to produce highly motivated skilled managers and technicians and, at the same time, provide upward opportunities for large numbers of marginalized workers (Keyfitz 1991; OECD 1996A, B).

Co-op education runs counter to competitive ideology. It involves teachers, students, and the public and private sectors in collaboration, based on trust and mutual benefit. Feedback from participants is enthusiastic because it establishes one-to-one relationships that are not typically found in modern mass education.

In co-op a basic theory of learning is implemented that engages students and mentors interactively, producing symbolically meaningful relations. There is a closer bond between actors than in traditional teaching. Co-op integrates learning by combining the abstract with the concrete. This happens through experiential learning.[2] In this approach students' interests and private knowledge are brought into contact with larger pools of knowledge through group experience.

Critics of traditional education argue that it is not value-free but, to the contrary, perpetuates stratification and inequality of opportunity.[3] One instrument for ensuring this outcome is streaming into fateful channels in Grade Nine, when students are in early adolescence. In North America the two streams are usually placed in different classrooms and sometimes different buildings on the basis of presumed ability for abstract thought. Those with "superior ability" are groomed for university. Courses from Grade Nine on are distinguished by their level of difficulty as part of the sorting process.

Defenders of the early segmentation of students into hierarchical programs claim that it stimulates students towards high achievement and rewards them while keeping the door open for late bloomers. Research into the high dropout rate throws serious doubt on this reasoning (Lawton and Leithwood 1988; Gamoran 1992; Crysdale and MacKay 1994; Radwanski 1987).

Conflict is inherent in competitive learning modes; the school allocates status and there are winners and losers (Anisef et al. 1982).[4] More democratic and open systems delay streaming until the later grades and then provide options as widely as possible. Ambition and enterprise in various forms are recognized and encouraged and the harsh consequences of cleavage at an early age between haves and have-nots are blunted.

In dealing with the transition from the subtle competitiveness of school to the cold competitiveness of the marketplace, co-op offers an alternative learning experience that prepares students positively for employment. Further, it increases the possibility of consonance between the values or goals held for youth by influential adults. When parents, educators, and employers together

encourage students to strive for attainable careers, they perform
better and have more self-confidence.

CHARACTERISTICS OF COOPERATIVE EDUCATION STUDENTS

Some educators have argued that co-op education is best suited to
young people who will not go on to post-secondary education
(Hruska 1973; A.J.C. King 1990). Others maintain that co-op
should prepare students for specific fields of work as it does at Canadian universities and colleges. However, there is increasing interest among secondary students in using co-op education as
career exploration. Thus, there has been a shift in the type of students who take the program. In the early 1980s the vast majority
of co-op students expected to leave school and go directly to work.
Since the program has become broadly legitimated, advanced-
level students also see co-op as a means to a variety of ends. However, taking two or more co-op credits reduces the number of general credits that might be required for admission to a college or
university. Advanced-level students, then, typically take a single academic co-op credit, while non-university-bound students link
multiple co-op credits to work-related credits in technology or
business. Hence co-op provides different experiences for the two
types of student.

It has been difficult to find placements in unionized settings because co-op students are seen sometimes to be doing work that
could be done by full-time union members. This restricts placements more for young men than for young women.

In Ontario co-op is typically offered as a double out-of-school
credit linked to a single credit in a school subject. But in Guelph
all students are encouraged to take co-op education, independent
of career aspirations or level of difficulty of the courses. In Peel
and Ottawa, non-university-bound students are primarily targeted
for co-op programs. Alberta makes available both short-term
work-study and co-op, or work experience, for all students regardless of social background and destination.

Across the country approximately 60 percent of co-op students
are female. This follows from their wider response to helpfulness
in preparing for work and from the fact that placements are more
available in typical female occupations, for example, clerking in

stores, clerical work in offices, and assisting in social service. The proportion of placements in skilled trades, unionized firms, and typically male occupations is lower.

Achievement can be judged in two ways: by the level of difficulty at which students take their courses and by the marks they obtain. The former has traditionally been regarded as the most useful criterion for high-level students bound for post-secondary education. Table 5–1 shows that a majority of sample youth enrolled in co-op were likely to take courses at a non-university-bound level.

Fewer co-op students receive marks at the higher and lower ends of the scale. This is because marks attained by non-university-bound students tend to be more homogeneous, that is, average rather than high or low. Moreover, few low-achieving students are encouraged or allowed to take co-op since in many schools the opportunity is given only to students who have shown they can act responsibly in work settings.

Co-op students are still apt to come from lower-status homes. They are also more likely to come from Anglo-Saxon families. Non-Anglos tend to think that academic programs lead to better jobs.

The non-co-op students in the sample were somewhat more likely to make a moderate effort (39 percent compared with 33 percent for co-op students), and co-op students were more likely to say they made a great effort (19 as compared with 14 percent of non-co-op students).

How do co-op students adjust to the labour market? We tested the effects of co-op, or work experience through the following aspects of adjustment: extent of unemployment, level of wages, job status, worries over job search, and intrinsic satisfaction with job (see chapter 8). Eleven percent of our sample were still at school when we interviewed them, more non-co-op than co-op.

One-half of both the co-op and non-co-op youth had been unemployed at least once since leaving school, with very little difference in the number of times. However, non-co-op youth had longer periods of unemployment. The co-op youth who ranked the program most favourably were those who had been the most consistently employed of the entire sample. Co-op students were more likely to earn higher wages at this early stage of employment. They were less likely to occupy high-level jobs but more

Table 5–1
Level of Courses Taken by Co-op and Non-Co-op Students (Percentages)

	Co-op	Non-co-op
University bound	26.5	49.3
Non-university bound	73.5	50.7

likely to have middle-level jobs. Overall, the difference is not significant. Co-op students who evaluated the program as very helpful had better jobs than other co-op cohorts.

Former co-op students were less likely to worry about lack of experience and training, getting a good job, where to look for work, and the need for good connections – all job orientations. However, they were slightly more worried about the chance of being rejected, their personalities, and their levels of education – personal and status orientations.

Accumulated research indicates that intrinsic satisfaction is a stronger correlate of striving and performance than extrinsic satisfaction (King et al. 1979; Ninalowa 1983). The former is based on a sense of achievement, responsibility, and freedom in performing tasks and the latter is based on benefits that are by-products of the tasks: pay, security, and conditions. Fifty-four percent of the sample youth who were working full time found intrinsic satisfaction in their jobs. This did not vary between former co-op and non-co-op students.

EFFECTIVENESS OF COOP EDUCATION

Ninety-one percent of former co-op students said they would take the program again. And half of non-co-op interviewees said they would take the program if they were to start afresh (cf. Heinemann 1981; Finch et al. 1991).

Table 5–2 presents the proportion of co-op youth who rated aspects of the program as "very helpful." The highest ratings were for relations with employers, understanding the work world, and the quality and content of teaching. Over one-half gained substantially in self-confidence and over one-quarter improved their school performance as a result of the program. This remark was typical: "My grades increased from Cs to Bs that year."

Table 5–2
Percentage of Youth Who Rated Co-op Education "Very Helpful"

Relations with employers	71
Learned applied skills	62
Effective teaching	62
Better understanding of work	59
Course content	58
More self-confidence	54
Helping to get a job	48
Choosing a career	44
Smooth passage into work	37
Improved school performance	28

Asked why they took co-op education, 18 percent of youth gave negative or neutral reasons – they were not interested in academic subjects, not good at them, or they followed others' suggestions. The remaining 82 percent gave positive reasons – they wished to explore careers or learn about jobs.

Generally speaking, those who participated in co-op felt accepted in their workplace settings. A fine arts co-op student said: "It was surprising. Everybody was so nice, which I almost didn't expect, because these are people with degrees. And they were surprised that someone so young would be interested already in doing something like interior design. The first thing they showed me was the library at the back. My God, it was so overwhelming! They got me doing filing at first because getting to know the library would be getting to know them and their work."

Over half of former co-op students indicated that the program raised their self-confidence and improved their capacity to grasp new opportunities. A co-op drafting student said: "It's been quite a year. I've completely switched around. My expectations of myself have increased because I can see that I can accomplish the things I set out to do. I believe I've made a good choice. It's been the best experience of my life. I was accepted by the university for first year architecture. It was a surprise. A year ago I wouldn't have thought myself capable of something like that. Now I know I can do it."

Modest parental education and jobs and the absence of consonance between the aspirations of parents, teachers, and early employers did not keep some advanced level students from completing Grade Twelve. After a co-op course, one student in this situation found a good position with a financial firm. Co-op helped her to develop skills that led to a promotion and the prospect of advancement to management. "It brought me out of my shell and by the time the course finished, I had a lot of confidence."

Increasing numbers of high school students, as stated earlier, viewed co-op as career preparation. For some, both general goals and occupational preparation are achieved. "Although the project didn't turn out the way I thought it would, I am grateful I had the chance to experience the life of a writer. I will be more ready to work at it when the time comes. In fact, because of this co-op course I was chosen for another at the Great Canadian Theatre Company."

Youth with strong support at home, usually with parents as examples, whose career aims were high, and who made a good effort at school found co-op to be very useful. An advanced student in science was placed in a university physics department. This led to chemistry honours at university and a job as a Class 1 medical technologist while he was writing his thesis. He's always worked during the school year, though not more than 20 hours a week. He failed a high school computer course and took a dislike to such courses. But at university he "embraced" them and wants to have a career that links computers with chemistry.

I learned a lot about physics through co-op and it introduced me to a different academic world. It really made my career goals clearer and it taught me research skills. Before that I couldn't connect school with my ultimate aims.

As for the purpose of secondary education, the first is to learn how to study and discipline yourself, then develop some applied skills, in my case, in research. It happens through socialization. Also high school should help you choose a goal; otherwise why study? What happens is empowerment – to gain as much knowledge as possible. Co-op can focus this. I transferred from a small rural school so that I could do this and take sciences. I owe a lot to my teachers, especially the one who approved my placement.

Another advanced-level student decided in Grade Twelve to become an elementary teacher. Her co-op course led to part-time supply teaching as soon as she graduated from university and that resulted in a full-time appointment.

At a more modest level, some co-op students give the program credit for leading to skilled or supervisory jobs. Although they had not gone past Grade Nine, one girl's parents encouraged her and her brothers to complete community college. From her teens she wanted to work with disadvantaged children. A co-op course in Grade Twelve led to a college diploma and she is now an aide in a special education class. She plans to get a BA and become a teacher. "I really enjoyed both the classes and fieldwork. I'm not really a high academic achiever but performed well. That got me into college. We had a wonderful high school teacher who visited us at the workplace. Having hands-on experience, the college program was much more meaningful. I didn't walk out puzzled and saying, hmm!"

For many youth, co-op education is a way of exploring careers. Those who take co-op in secondary school often end up working in a different area. One young woman expected that she would go into daycare work for handicapped children but after a co-op course decided it was not for her. She changed direction to take a BSc degree and start work as a therapist in a seniors' home.

A comparative survey found that co-op students were more likely to find placements in high- to middle-skilled jobs (Heffren 1998).

IMPROVING CO-OP PROGRAMS

Youth   While former co-op students generally liked the program, some saw room for improvement, for example, in the low level of work often assigned. One girl's placement was unchallenging but it led to something better. Another girl suggested students be given more difficult tasks such as writing analytical reports instead of simple descriptive journals.

Parents and teachers   Forty-two percent of parents in our sample said they knew little or nothing about co-op, 36 percent had a general idea, and 23 percent had detailed information. In fact, few of the youth in the class of 1984–85 knew much about co-op. Many wished they had known more since it would have raised their interest in school.

Table 5–3
Parents' and Teachers' Views on Co-op Education (Percentages)

	Parents	Teachers
1 Advantages of co-op education?		
None, don't know, no answer	16	16
Keeps students in school, encourages them	11	13
Provides work experience	68	67
Other	5	5
	100	101
2 Disadvantages of co-op education?		
None, don't know	46	28
Lowers academic performance, cuts study time	16	10
Problems with screening, monitoring, etc.	24	32
Organizational problems	14	30
	100	100
3 Should co-op be expanded to include most students?		
No	20	21
Yes, those in difficulty	6	12
Yes, to a wide range of students	62	56
Other replies	13	10
	101	99

Table 5–3 compares the views of parents and teachers on co-op education. Teachers are more precise as they are directly involved. Their views vary with specialization and philosophy.

Regarding what is right about the program, co-op is viewed similarly by parents and teachers. Table 5–3 shows more variance in defining its problems. These include screening students and employers and monitoring conditions and performance, where the close experience of teachers is evident. One-third of teachers stress operation and another third think of organizational problems such as timetabling, staffing, and supervision.

There is more agreement on the future; most parents and teachers favour the expansion of cooperative education to include a wide range of students in terms of level of difficulty as well as subject concentration.

Of the sample teachers involved in work-study or co-op education, 83 percent felt that a wide range of students benefit from work education, 13 percent thought that all students might benefit, and five percent think the programs help mostly students at low levels and underachievers. Among non-co-op teachers, 85 percent agreed that a wide range of students should take the program, four percent said all students should, and 11 percent would focus on low performers. Most would not permit students below Grade Eleven to take co-op because they lack maturity and responsibility.

Employers According to employers, 52 percent of students, co-op or non-co-op, are given unskilled positions such as counter help, file clerks, or material handlers, while 44 percent are in semiskilled work like bookkeeping, simple machine operation, or driving. Only four percent hold skilled jobs such as junior drafting and apprenticeships. The latter require several years of training.

At the unskilled level, 45 percent of firms place or hire workers with less than Grade Twelve schooling, 50 percent require Grade Twelve, and five percent require more education. For the few skilled jobs available to secondary students, only 12 percent of employers accept candidates with less than Grade Twelve education, 28 percent need Grade Twelve, and 60 percent require more than Grade 12.

Employers who had both co-op and non co-op students generally rated the two groups similarly in attitude to work, appearance, productivity, quality of work and communication skills. Ratings did not vary systematically with size of firm, region or gender of respondent. Public agencies and technical service firms gave somewhat higher scores for co-op education workers than firms in other sectors. Technical services include medical clinics, surveyors, graphics specialists, and computer consultants.

WORK-STUDY STUDENTS

The number of young people who took work-study (a two- to four-week block within a course) was too small for significance analysis. Nevertheless, it is useful to compare their experiences with those of co-op students and those who did not participate at all in work-education.

Although work-study youth had employment patterns similar to other groups, they tended to make less money and were less satisfied with their jobs. They were also more worried about get-

ting a good job, lack of experience, personality, chance of rejection, and competition. Overall, the work-study group had less
success than the other two groups in early transition to work. We
cannot say how much of their disadvantage was due to pre-
existing factors.

CHAPTER SIX

Employers and Transition

Because education usually holds centre stage in discussions of transition, research has tended to neglect the essential role of employers. North American societies, we have noted, tend to separate education and employment. This is particularly so in Canada where jurisdiction over education is allocated to the provinces and that over employment and training to the federal government. In the last few years, with awakening concern over transition and training, governments and educators have initiated changes to bridge the gap between school and work. Strangely, most employers are minor players. As pointed out in chapter 5, only a small minority have adequate training programs or participate in such efforts as cooperative education.

Richard Marquardt (1996, 14) shows that Canada's educational system is comparatively open, facilitating movement back and forth between it and employment. "At the same time weak connections with the labour market put a great deal of pressure on individuals to make risky choices about education and to take responsibility for their own skill training. The danger is that this will result in high levels of job-education mismatch and lengthy trial-and-error searching for favourable outcomes."

The groundswell of the information age is radically changing the nature of work. In this upheaval, employers and educators must face the question "What should youth be prepared for?" One thing is certain – that good, high-tech jobs will be available only for those who are well prepared in skills and general knowledge, bonding cognition with theory, imagination with commitment. As educators and employers work together, youth can claim the best of the new age. But large numbers will not make it, thanks partly to entrenched social barriers and the slow pace of collaboration between most educators and employers.

While the pool of well educated work entrants is swelling, a high proportion of old jobs in service sectors, where most people still work, are being replaced or destabilized. In *Whose Brave New World?* Heather Menzies (1996) predicts that the workforce will soon consist of two groups. The smaller one will have steady jobs, using new technologies, while the larger one will have temporary, insecure, more or less menial jobs (Gooderham 1995). Nathan Keyfitz (1991) at the International Centre for Technological Research in Lausanne, reaches a similar conclusion.

In *The Canadian Workplace in Transition*, Gordon Betcherman and associates (1994A: 76) observe that "job security has deteriorated generally with the advance of foreign competition and industrial technology. OECD (1993) found that countries with low-tenure jobs tend to be those with less workplace training. Canadian workers "often do not have the opportunity to enhance their employment security by upgrading skills in current jobs."

In Canada the average job tenure is eight years, compared with nearly 11 years in Japan and seven in the United States. Tenure exceeds the Canadian level in Germany, Switzerland, France, and Finland.

Moreover, non-standard employment such as part-time and temporary work increased between 1975 and 1993 from 23.6 to 30 percent of the total workforce (Betcherman et al., 1994, 76).

On-the-job training in Canada is apt to be provided for employees between the ages of 24 and 55, who have post-secondary or university education and who earn $35,000 a year or more (ibid. 79).

The new economy calls for changes in human resource management. It is now conventional wisdom that human resources are the key to success in the increasingly competitive high-technology environment. In contrast, Canadian firms typically base their strategies on cutting costs by introducing new technologies without retraining workers (ibid., 91).

Partly as a result of the widespread lack of technical preparation, youth workers under 25 are experiencing relative disadvantages in employment and pay. The unemployment rate rose in the

1980s and early 1990s to 16.2 percent, according to the OECD (1993), compared with 4.5 percent in Japan, 6.1 in Sweden, and 6.4 in Germany. It was higher than the Canadian rate in Australia, France, Italy, and Spain but somewhat lower in the United Kingdom and the US, 12.9 percent each (Betcherman and Morissette 1994B).

Average hourly wages of those aged 16 to 24 fell as a percentage of wages for individuals aged 25 to 64, from 83.1 for men in 1981 to 74.5, and for women, from 87.0 percent in 1981 to 81.4 in 1988 (ibid., Table 13).

Polarization of wages also increased during the same time period and has continued since. Again, the spread was greater among men and, perhaps surprisingly, it was wider among men with university degrees than among those with less education. And those under 25 bore the brunt of the decline in earnings (Morissette et al. 1995).

Against this backdrop of rapid basic change we now discuss the interaction of employers with educators and youth. We compare the present job levels of young people with their aspirations and look at sectors of employment, the fit between school and work, on-the-job training, guidance and counselling, relations with schools, employers' involvement in co-op education, correlates of employers' hopes for youth, job-hunt worries, unemployment, and part-time jobs. Some of these issues are touched on elsewhere; here they are treated together as components of the working world of youth.

THE PERSPECTIVE OF YOUTH

Despite their high hopes, most of our sample youth, five years out of high school, were working at relatively low-level jobs. This is shown in Table 6–I. The difference between those who had low-level job hopes in Grade Ten (one percent), those whose job hopes remained low once they'd started working (two percent), and those who are in fact working at unskilled or semi-skilled jobs (35 percent) is startling. That 11 percent of the sample were still at college or university does not account for the difference. In short, *many young adults still had unrealistic hopes.*

Almost one-half of the youth sample, 47.5 percent, were or had been working in service sectors – personal, financial, technical, and

Table 6–1
Job Aspirations in Grade Ten, Present Expectations, and Present Status
(Percentages)

	Aspirations in Grande 10	Present Expectations	Present Job
Unskilled, semi-skilled	1	2	35
Skilled blue- and white-collar	25	25	31
Manager, small firm; supervisor, medium-size firm	10	18	11
Manager, medium-size firm; owner, professional	30	49	7
No plans, don't know, not in workforce	34	7	17*
Totals	100	101	101
Frequencies	(293)	(320)	(324)

* Six percent of the youth sample were looking for work and 11 percent were students.

public. Most of these, 34 percent, worked in personal services (foods, catering, accommodation, and grooming). Five percent were in construction, 13 percent each in manufacturing and transport/communication, and nearly 16 percent were in merchandising, while six percent were registered as unemployed, far fewer than in the population overall. The largest proportion of jobs were insecure, often part time, and usually brought in low wages.

Half of the sample youth believe that education should prepare them for employment, but half also said that there was no relation between their schooling and employment. Twenty-four percent said that there was a partial fit while only 26 percent said that there was a good fit. Further, among the 80 percent of those former high school students who had held part-time jobs during term, four-fifths said that their jobs had had no connection with their schooling or career plans. Disjunction on such a large scale contributes to disorder in transition.

For the lucky minority for whom school courses and desired jobs were closely related, there were many benefits (Table A–10). These include strong effort at school, help from friends, more education, higher marks, better jobs, intrinsic satisfaction with their present jobs, better pay, innovativeness, high hopes by employers for the youth's education, consonance among parents, teachers, and employers for educational and occupational goals, and general satisfaction. Fewer of these former students were unemployed and fewer worried over finding work.

Youth whose schooling and jobs matched were also apt to attend religious services. This legitimates and integrates values and behaviour.

Co-op students are more likely than others to experience a close fit between courses and early jobs. This is one of the goals of the program and, no doubt, a strong reason for its popularity.

Guidance and counselling were not discussed in the chapter on education because former students rarely mentioned it as a factor in transition. Very few said school-based counsellors helped. In a survey of Swedish cohorts a small but significant proportion gave work counsellors and teachers credit for helping them choose upper secondary programs that led to better-than-average jobs (Crysdale et al. 1998).

In northwestern Europe educators and employers have collaborative programs of guidance and counselling. Sectorial groups of employers work closely with schools and colleges to provide counselling and training. Young adults report that they are helpful.

National structures differ according to basic values. In the UK the market-driven labour system is reflected in sharply tiered routes to employment after school. But in Sweden, with its equalitarian inclination, education at the upper levels is open until the final years, when it becomes highly specialized and closely related to industry and business. The British and Swedish examples are discussed in chapter 9. In Canada counselling is focused in secondary school where, according to most former students, it is usually minimal and impersonal.

[Where] much or most work is becoming less routine, workers will need above all to respond flexibly to changing demands, to solve problems, to take responsibility and to work in teams with relatively flat hierarchies. General education may provide a better preparation for young people to learn skills at later stages of the occupational career ... On the other hand vocational skills are a better preparation for transition into employment ... Thus a tension is created between the need for [both] ... This can be addressed through greater convergence between general and work-oriented learning ...

Good guidance can reduce unemployment by improving the fit between the knowledge and skills of individuals and opportunities ... on the labour market. A further potential benefit is the upgrading of the workforce ... a consequent increase in job satisfaction and, possibly, a reduction of inequality of opportunity. (OECD 1996B, 147)

A typically Canadian compromise lies in co-op education, while young people are at upper high school or post-secondary levels. Youth who were in co-op were more satisfied with the guidance and counselling they received.

Worries and Unemployment

Segmentation of the labour force is starkly evident in the experience of youth at low levels, marked by worry in job hunting and unemployment. We asked youth how worried they would be in searching for work and show responses in Table 6–2. Worries focus on job quality, inexperience, and competition.

The replies were scored as follows for each item: (0) not at all worried, (1) a little worried, (2) quite worried. Scores for the ten items were added to form the scale "Job-Hunt Worries."

The social status of parents, gender, ethnicity, and most intermediate outcomes such as others' educational aspirations for their education had no effect on the level of youth's worries about job hunting. Most youth worry to some extent (see Hasan and de Broucker 1984). However, positive transitional factors did significantly reduce anxiety, as Table A–11 shows.

Less effort by students led to lower marks, less education, lower hopes by employers for their advancement, less intrinsic work satisfaction, lower pay, and fewer innovative plans. Less effort also led to a higher level of job-hunt anxiety, which was exacerbated by long periods of unemployment (cf. Weiss 1990). Failure in transition, like success, is a cumulative process.

The 1982 recession marked a watershed in youth unemployment, as mentioned in the preface. The official rate jumped beyond 18 percent, nearly double that for workers aged 25 and over. It has remained high for 15 years – 17 percent in January 1997, still about twice the rate for older workers. The real rate is much higher, since many without adequate education or training have

Table 6–2
Job-Hunt Worries (Percentages)

	Not worried	A little worried	Quite worried
Getting a good job	24	43	33
Lack of experience	25	44	31
Competition for the job	22	50	28
Chance of rejection	32	46	22
Not enough education	48	31	20
Lack of training	44	39	17
Where to look, what to do	52	34	14
Having good connections	48	41	12
Getting good references	79	17	4
Personality	73	23	4

given up looking or registering (cf. Krahn and Lowe 1991, 146; Marquardt 1996, 14–20; Spain et al. 1991).

The woes of *prolonged* unemployment are depressing, as Table A–12 demonstrates. Youth who experience prolonged unemployment did not find the early support and encouragement that are usually necessary for a positive transition. Those whose mothers had high-level occupations were not often unemployed; nor were those whose fathers helped them strongly.

Similarly, those who earned good marks were less likely to be unemployed, along with those who had high aspirations and whose teachers and employers had high hopes for them. The strongest predictor of unemployment is a low level of education ($r = -.261$).

From Table A–12 we learn that prolonged unemployment is accompanied by intense job-hunt worries. Those with better jobs are less unemployed, as are those who think technology is positive for their future.

Part-time Work during Term

Work becomes important to most youth once they reach 16, the legal age for working and for leaving school. Eighty-two percent of

Table 6–3
Youth's Views on the Effects of Work during Term (Percentages)

	No effects	Some interference	Considerable interference
On studying and marks	58	28	15
On school activities	62	24	14
On social life	63	27	10
On family life	81	15	4

our sample worked part time while in secondary school, 38 percent for two years or less, 45 percent for three or four years, and 17 percent for over four years.

As Table 6–3 shows, a majority felt that their jobs had no ill effects on their school, social, or family life. The mean time spent on part-time work was 19.4 hours. Students who worked over 16 hours attained less education and said that work did interfere with their studies, school activities, and social life. Co-op students put in shorter hours at part-time jobs than others.

The main purpose of part-time jobs was to earn money, occasionally out of necessity but more commonly to support a consumerist lifestyle. The youth market is huge in Western societies, creating a vast demand for modish clothing, recreation, music, vehicles, fast foods, and sports. The media have generated a gratifying lifestyle for youth, replete with complex status-building paraphernalia.

For many youth part-time work has supplanted school-based extracurricular activities, community participation, and enriched family life. For a minority it provides financial security, an identity, and peer support they do not find in adult-oriented institutions.

The debate about the effects of part-time work during the school term is vigorous. Some argue that, on balance, it is harmful for transition (Greenberger and Steinberg 1986; Marsh 1991). Others conclude that working during high school years overall has mixed or minimal effects on full-time employment (Mortimer and Finch 1986). But few models specify the number of hours the students spend working. Teachers in our study believe that long hours at part-time work depress school performance, and research supports this contention (Gilbert et al. 1993).

Most parents tacitly approve of young people working part time since they believe it fosters responsibility and independence (cf. D'Amico 1984; Mortimer and Finch 1986). For low-income families, additional earnings are a boon. In any case, youth over-whelmingly adopt it as a normal part of growing up in North America.

On balance, long hours spent during term on part-time work that is unrelated to schooling has a negative effect on transition to a technologized workforce. In a 16-year project in Eastside, a working-class area in Toronto, it was found that youth who spent long hours at part-time jobs unrelated to school reached lower levels in education and job entry (Crysdale and MacKay 1994).

The trend towards part-time work as a permanent feature of the labour market contributes to segmentation between jobs that are "good" or "bad" with respect to pay, security, intrinsic satisfaction, and prospects. In all these measures part-time work for long hours, unrelated to schooling and careers, scores badly, especially for women. Yet most new jobs in the general service sector are temporary and part time (cf. Marquardt 1996, 22).

Five years after high school, 20 percent of our youth sample were still employed part time. Another 61 percent worked full time; almost half their posts were unskilled or semi-skilled, with limited horizons in advancement and fulfilment. Some four percent of youth were working both full and part time. Another 15 percent were not in the labour force.[2]

The mean pay for part-time work was $169 a week. Thirty-five percent earned $100 or less, and a similar proportion earned over $200. In contrast, the mean weekly pay for full-time work was $440, with about one-third earning under $350 a week and an-other one-third $450 or more. One young man of Oriental origin, manager of a small firm and partly self-employed, reported a weekly income of over $1,000. He was a university graduate.

THE PERSPECTIVE OF EMPLOYERS

Training: The Great Canadian Handicap

Canadian employers acknowledge that one of their chief concerns in meeting severe offshore competition is the shortage of well-trained staff. Yet they spend on training only half the proportion

spent by United States firms (Canadian Labour Market and Productivity Centre 1990; Evers 1990). While Canada's rank in overall
competitiveness has risen to fourth from eighth in a world survey
from 1996 to 1997, the chief reason is not training but a decrease
in the deficit (World Economic Forum 1997). Firms in Canada also
spend much less than average on research and development[3]
(Conference Board of Canada 1995A).

Universities now have less public funding for research and, in
recent years, have produced fewer doctorates than before in
science, maths, engineering, and applied sciences. The prospects
of improving productivity dim as fewer youth will enter university
in the next decade for various reasons, including rising fees.

Canada has traditionally relied on immigration to a large extent
to meet the demand for skilled workers. Since the 1982 recession
and the rapid growth in demand for skills, efforts have been
increased to expand and update training. For several reasons,
however, including the jurisdictional allocation of education to
provinces and employment and training to the federal state, Canada has fallen behind other countries in training and retraining.
In Sweden, particularly, training has been at the centre of manpower policy. This has been a key to their notable growth and productivity (Tully 1988).

Recent conferences of employers have expressed concern over
shortages of skilled workers and the absence of effective measures
to deal with them. Software technologists say there is a shortage for
12,000 jobs and the gap will reach 20.000 by the year 2000
(Brethour 1997). And automotive parts manufacturers warn of severe impending shortages of skilled workers (Keenan 1997). Immigration cannot fill the gap as well as long-term training of youth.
Training establishes links between entrants and agencies that foster
further upgrading as new technologies emerge (Meltz 1988).

Of 277 firms in the sample, 40 percent have no training program for new full-time entrants, 10 percent say workers learn
informally on the job, and 50 percent offer some form of training.
Thirteen percent have programs that last less than one week,
14 percent have programs of one week to one month, and only
22 percent have longer programs.

Fifteen percent of the firms have apprentices; seven percent
have three or more. This is higher than the proportion across

Canada. Most firms with apprentices are in transportation, communication, or manufacturing. These figures do not include employees who are taking accounting or other courses off the job, usually on their own time and at their own expense.

Most employers offering training are in public services such as health care, or in technical services. The former are likely to offer training on the job, while technical firms combine such training with sponsored courses off the job. Larger establishments offer longer programs. Firms involved in co-op education are more likely to offer formal courses and these are longer than elsewhere.

Not all observers agree that job training in Canada is deficient. Constantine Kapsalis (1993) maintains that it compares favourably with what is done in most advanced countries in the OECD. Drawing on the 1991 Adult Education and Training Survey (1993), he reports that 30 percent of workers participated in employer-sponsored programs and another 18 percent in unsponsored courses. This rate is surpassed only in Great Britain, Finland, and Japan. However, the time spent by trainees in courses put on by Canadian employers averages just over eight working days in the year, and just over 12 days in unsponsored courses. Training in advanced European systems generally lasts much longer and is centred chiefly at work sites closely coordinated with schools and communities.

Kapsalis concludes that attention should be shifted from accessibility to the quality of training. Our study indicates that both accessibility and quality need to be addressed.

Efforts in these directions are being undertaken by provincial and federal governments. The Youth Employment Strategy, offered by the federal Ministry of Human Resources Development as of 1997 with a budget of two billion dollars, coordinates and streamlines youth initiatives. It includes the unemployed and those without adequate education or training and works with schools, employers, and community groups.

Also in 1997 the Ontario Ministry of Education and Training began the Career and Employment Preparation Program, aimed at out-of-work and out-of-school youth, with a budget of $110 million. It offers three services: Information and Referral, Planning Preparation, and On-the-Job Training. It is client-oriented and more accessible than earlier programs, and it subsidizes wages for qualified entrants, one-third of whom are social assistance recipients. Evaluation and accountability are built into the design.

Other provinces and the territories are moving in a similar direction. Saskatchewan in 1997 is spending $131,000,000 on training, picking up the slack resulting from retrenchment by the federal government. Employers work with colleges and institutes to provide more training in the workplace with its new equipment (J. Lewington 1997).

Employers' Relations with Schools

Thirty-seven percent of sample employers think that their relations with schools are weak, 46 percent see them as moderate, and only 17 percent call them strong. Small firms with fewer than 20 employees are less involved, as Table 6–4 shows. Most employers have suggestions for strengthening relations with schools, whether or not they are involved with co-op education. Public agencies and technical service firms have closer ties with schools; they also place the highest value on co-op. Merchants and personal service firms are not keen on ties with schools, co-op education, or training. In our sample they were the largest employers of youth with little education.

For example, the many departmental supervisors in one large automotive and general merchant firm are not much better educated than ordinary clerks and not much better paid. Higher status is the main reward for advancement. Fast-food chains hold brief training sessions to foster efficiency and pleasant manners. They don't need better educated workers but still have hierarchies of positions.

Among workers with few qualifications, low-quality jobs, little security, and poor prospects, many say that, in compensation, they enjoy their relations with others at work and some prefer not to compete for advancement.

There are systematic variations in training between regions. Firms in Ottawa and Peel have more technical jobs and provide longer training. Those in Ottawa and Guelph are more involved with co-op education and emphasize training. Because Alberta requires that students take at least one course in work education, Edmonton has higher student participation than other areas.

Table 6–4
Employers' Views on Relations with Schools by Size of Firm (Percentages)

	Small Firms (Under 20 employees)	Medium-size (20–100 employees)	Large Firms (Over 100 employees)	All Firms
Weak	41	40	13	37
Moderate	46	40	59	46
Strong	13	19	28	17
Total %	100	99	100	100
Frequencies	(145)	(72)	(39)	(257)

The Cumulative Effects of Employer Aspirations for Youth

When employers take a sustained interest in students, correlations with positive outcomes are strong. This applies particularly to youth's educational and career goals. Our data are based on youth's perceptions, which are real and consequential. Young people who have advantaged family backgrounds acknowledge more than others the help and encouragement of early employers. The impact of these influential "others" is cumulative and powerful (see chapter 8).

There is a fairly strong correlation between parental and employer aspirations for youth's careers ($r = .346$), and young people themselves remark on similarities between what their parents and early employers hope for them, whether high or low. Another solid correlation is that between employers' and youth's own career aspirations ($r = .358$). Encouragement by employers is also related with actual attainment ($r = .227$). Educational attainment is driven by career goals, although to some extent these variables are reciprocal.

In popular culture, prestige is high for those whose jobs support an affluent lifestyle. Few can escape or wish to escape the allure of a materialist marketplace. This is qualified, however, by the persistent wish among a majority of youth for intrinsic satisfaction at work, with attributes of freedom, responsibility, and meaningfulness.

Logically and empirically, the end goal – a good job – drives the intermediate goal – a good education. This helps us understand why most students think that the primary purpose of education should be the building of social and applied skills.

Employers' Views on Transition

Employers' views on transition are coloured by level of computer-ization and their degree of participation in co-op programs. Those using new technologies are more concerned with education and training and more apt to take part in co-op programs. When em-ployers talk of schools, many refer to co-op (cf. chapter 5).

Firms with positive views A film producer says, "Students actually assist in production, and we give them credit in the film – even novices. They keep expenses down, too. Co-op is the greatest thing around; I did it myself a few years ago and now I'm in man-agement. Filming takes artistic talent and college courses can't teach that: students have to learn by working. Teachers and coun-sellors should get out of the classroom and observe in the work-place."

A general hospital has increased placements for co-op students, who now log 7,000 hours per year. A supervisor says, "Most kids are well prepared. They have half a day at school and half a day here under supervision. Applicants must meet certain require-ments; most have well-prepared CVs, are well groomed and present themselves well. It's a good experience for them and for us."

A mid-size graphics firm places high school as well as college students. The manager says, "Some younger ones, in Grade Twelve, are talented in art; others learn technical skills. The better ones, who are committed and enthusiastic, go to college and we hire some of them back. Co-op works well if teachers are not too rigid in expectations, as we have to place entrants where we need them and where they can contribute. Teachers we work with are very open and supportive."

A firm that installs security systems rates co-op "150 percent." Supervisors prefer co-op students: "They are well prepared and screened. It's like hiring through a good agency. We train them, although I know of firms that use them as cheap labour. Schools should advertise the program more. Not only do we help the kids through training and pay for overtime and holiday hours; they help us."

A diesel engineering firm strongly supports co-op as a way of re-lating to schools and finding potential employees. The manager says: "Most educators overemphasize academic studies and down-grade trades. Parents and teachers tell students not to become grease monkeys and some of them end up sweeping floors. Many kids could have a bright future in technical areas, but how do you convince their teachers?"

A computer service firm places handicapped students. "It's a community service but also improves our relations with the health systems. The brief hours at present are a disadvantage. It would be better if students could be with us four months and then at school four months, as in some university co-op programs."

A supervisor in a large sales firm says: "Co-op should start earlier, so that upper secondary students are better able to choose courses and careers that go together. We have much to learn from northern European systems. We hire full-time some excellent students who started with co-op."

A municipal department hires between 400 and 1,000 part-time workers, depending on the season. The manager tries to give co-op students non-menial jobs where training is required. Some are assigned to office jobs, others help technicians, planners, and engineers. They have better attitudes than non-co-op students, though usually they're at the same skill level.

Firms with reservations A large sales firm has had a different experience. The manager finds that some students take the view that because they are not paid, they will have an easier time. "Relations with schools, accordingly, are not the best, but we persist, as some co-op people are excellent and have been given full-time jobs later. It depends more on personality and ability than grade level, in our case."

A medium-size firm that makes truck bodies has a few co-op students but most of its inexperienced help are non-co-op. "When they're paid, we have more control over them. Students start at menial levels, then may move up to do some semi-skilled work such as light welding. One young fellow started as a cleaner and ended as foreman. Because the skill level has risen with more technology, we no longer train trades people. Co-op students have the opportunity to observe at close hand and, if interested, may go on themselves to get certificates."

A firm that trains air crew used co-op students extensively at one time, but schools were not keeping up with technology so the program has gone downhill. The supervisor can't understand why schools are not familiarizing students with Lotus software, which is used by most businesses. "There has to be more interaction and input from business in shaping school programs. They spend too much time on books and are not realistic about the field."

Small firms Smaller firms have mixed views on their part in transition, due partly to limits in staff and training. A machine-shop operator thinks his firm's relations with schools are weak; their first co-op student was a dud. Nevertheless, he thinks the program is great; others have had success with it and he's willing to persist.

The head of a printing shop that has computerized equipment says it is difficult to find competent operators. "Our first co-op student had potential but wanted money more than training. I come from Europe where the schools give young workers a sound basic training. A revised apprentice system is the way to go."

Another small employer supports co-op, though it takes more of his time than he gets back. To strengthen weak relations with schools, employers should go into schools to talk with staff and students, as he does. Co-op, he believes, should be built into modern education.

Non-co-op firms Many firms with no experience in co-op are either confused about transition or pessimistic about solving the problem. The proprietor of a repair shop says: "Schools put too much emphasis on academic subjects and preparing professionals and not enough on skill training. We teach helpers on the job and then it's hard to keep them."

A small specialty food merchant says, "Honesty is lost by the time kids get to high school. They think they can get a free lunch. They don't realize there's a price to pay for achievement. We try to hire students but their attitude is all wrong."

A medium-size manufacturer says students face production jobs that are mostly mindless. One summer he had an engineering student who was excellent. Most of his supervisory staff work their way up the ladder.

One manager says, "Small businesses can't afford to train workers, and just now we're looking for a fitter-welder. It's hard to find skilled people. We need trade schools with longer-term programs than high schools offer. Students need academic education but also sufficient practical training to get started in a shop like ours."

A medium-size manufacturer doesn't need high tech equipment or training. According to the manager, "new workers, after observation and a few days' instruction, get on the assembly line and do it. Many kids have poor attitudes. They need most of all a willingness to work."

A small company that repairs technical equipment finds it hard to get good tradespeople. "Students in middle school in Europe spend several weeks in various work places," the owner says. "That gives them a chance to decide how to specialize in upper high school."

The manager of a silk-screen printshop uses robotic machines and needs few operators, but they must be skilled and this takes continual training. He has not had suitable co-op placements but believes it can work well.

An owner says that the only reason he has his business is because an early boss took the trouble to show him the necessary technical and management skills. He is willing to get involved in co-op and to act as a resource person in seminars at schools.

The supervisor of a specialized machine shop, a woman, had not heard of co-op education but likes the idea. "Our machines are complex and require a fairly high level of training before employment. It's best for schools not to specialize too much but to provide basics in general and applied subjects, then in the last year or two they should be highly specialized, as they are in some European countries. Kids here are left on their own and many bright ones are left out."

One entirely computerized office that has not been involved in co-op would gladly take part. The supervisor says, "Willingness and ability to learn are more important than experience. Schools should adapt to work environments to help youth get a good start."

Another firm's spokesperson says, "Drawing the line between theory and practice is difficult; in co-op there is enough flexibility for schools and employers to do this together."

With leadership from ministries of Education and Training and local boards of education there could be a rapid development in the pool of students with skills to meet the needs of changing businesses. As one employer says, "Co-op really opens the eyes of young people. Some think it's going to be a snap at first, then are shocked to realize it's hard work. Some go on to achieve; others find it's not for them. How else can they learn this? Many go to university without a clue as to goals. Halfway through and facing imminent completion, they ask, 'What am I doing here and what will I do a couple of years from now?' Many graduates and job entrants still don't know."

CHAPTER SEVEN

Value Consonance
and Transition

THE FUNCTIONS OF CONSONANCE

The tendency towards consonance, or the ordering of behaviour into consistent patterns, is inherent in societies, which build systems of interaction that provide the continuity and predictability necessary for optimal existence. Why, then, in North America is there extensive disorder in the preparation of youth for adult productivity and status? Maladjustment arises to some extent from differences in opportunity for youth from various subcultures and classes. Where society is segmented on the basis of family inheritance or structured inequality, the rational and just distribution of opportunity often breaks down.

Most disprivileged youth remain in depressed economic and social strata, regardless of ability. There are exceptions. Some resist oversocialization and strive for autonomy. The individual aspects of transition are illustrated in the personal stories at the end of this chapter.

There is more predictability when consonance, or consensus, occurs in goals advised for youth by the major agents of socialization. This is a two-edged sword. For some it may heighten their drive and open opportunities. For others a lack of consonance among elders raises formidable barriers to advancement, psychically and structurally.

This reasoning goes beyond the concept of status crystallization (Lenski 1954), which posits a tendency towards consistency between the indicators of social class – education, occupation, and

income. Laura Starr (1987) was among the first to broaden the
concept and theorize that congruence between the goals of elders
and youth would lead to higher attainment. A common precondi-
tion for goal congruence is shared decision making.

In Table 7–1 we see that almost half of the youth sample
(48 percent) shared in decision making in the family. Participation declined to one-quarter at secondary school but rose again in
early jobs to almost one-half. The reduction at school is under-
standable: students are assembled into large classes by similarity
in age and social class in neighbourhood schools. There, most
youth think that decisions about goals, curricula, methods, and
specialization are typically made by elders or through random circumstances, with limited student participation.

To simplify analysis, we created a scale of overall consonance in
decision making by adding the scores for democratic process reported by youth at home, school, and work. Strong overall consonance in democratic decision making was reported by one-third
of the youth sample. Table 7–2 shows that while it did not occur
for most youth, consonance was strongest between family and
school (44 percent), declined between family and work (40 per
cent) and between school and work (37 percent). It was 34 percent between all three agents.

Young women reported having slightly less say than men. And
where parents had higher-than-average education, there was
stronger consonance; such young people expected and evoked
among teachers and employers a consultive form of decision-
making regarding careers. They learned at home how to consult.

However the process occurs, democratic decision making is
significantly related with positive intermediate factors such as
greater effort at school, high aspirations by others as well as by
self, and liberal gender norms. There is also a positive correlation
between consonance in decision making and final outcomes such
as education, present job, intrinsic satisfaction with ideal job, less
unemployment, and more innovative job planning.

This takes us to consonance in educational and job goals. Goals
express values or priorities. The positive effects of encouraging
the aspirations of youth have already been discussed. Here we
combine the aspirations for youth in schooling and jobs of the
three adult groups in our sample into the single measure "overall
consonance."

Table 7–1
Decision Making in the Family, at School, and at Work as Perceived
by Youth (Percentages)

	Family	School	Work
Mostly by elders	31	24	31
Little guidance	21	50	21
Democratically, with input from youth	48	27	48
Total %	100	101	100
Frequencies	(311)	(309)	(309)

Table 7–2
Strong Consensus in Democratic Decision Making between
Major Socialization Agents (Percentages)

Between family and school	44
Between family and work	40
Between school and work	37
Between all three agents	34

Table 7–3 shows that there was overall consensus between all three agents (in the bottom line of the table) for 44 percent of youth with respect to educational level but for only 18 percent in terms of job level. It is not surprising that there is a serious gap in the overall signals youth receive for future jobs, given what we learned in earlier chapters. Only 40 percent of parents conveyed to their children the hopes they had for their future positions, and only one-third of teachers and employers expressed their views. *There is an unwitting convergence of silence among most elders about careers for youth.*

There was strong consonance between parents and teachers in educational goals for 46 percent of youth and in job goals for 47 percent. The proportion fell for consonance between family and employers' goals for education, though it was somewhat greater again for jobs. In most cases the links between family, teachers, and employers for encouraging youth in job goals are weak.

Maternal occupation and the help mothers give their children are more strongly related with consonance than the occupations and helpfulness of fathers. Overall consonance has a fairly strong relationship with a youth's average marks, ultimate level of education,

Table 7–3
Overall Consonance among All Elders in Hopes for Youth's Education and
Job Level (Percentages)

	Education	Job Level
Between family and school	46	47
Between family and employers	27	39
Between school and employers	41	55
Between all three agents	44	18

and job goals. It also significantly affects the youth's effort at school, job level, intrinsic satisfaction with work, success at job training, and innovativeness. Youth whose elders strongly agree on goals are also less likely to be unemployed.

Hence there is convincing evidence that consonance improves a youth's chances of launching smoothly into work. The relative strength of consonance will be tested in the next chapter.

Weak consonance leads to a low self-image, lack of commitment, and less effort. This applies particularly to those whose parents are "disempowered" in class, ethnicity, or gender. Downgrading or silence by influential adults as to youth's potential is confusing and discouraging.

CAMEOS: EFFECTS OF CONSONANCE ON CAREER PLANNING

At the end of chapter 2 we developed a typology of youth's ideas on careers. Twenty-eight percent of our interviewees may be called *non-careerist, uncommitted,* or *uncertain* about their career plans. Another 35 percent are *conservative* – they wish to have established, secure careers. The remaining 38 percent are *innovative* – they plan on careers that change and require retraining from time to time. How did consonance in adult goals for youth affect their attitudes towards career planning?

Innovators

A young student in architecture was encouraged by her parents to go beyond high school but to make her own decisions about a career. They were both in positions of responsibility and were always taking courses. She took a co-op program in interior design, which she planned herself with the help of a co-op teacher. After this placement she switched to architecture. "I was more interested in the outside than the inside of buildings. This meant taking maths and physics in my last year at high school. I suddenly felt motivated and took three maths courses. To my surprise my grade average rose to 85 percent; it was in the 70s before. I quit my part-time job and really concentrated. Getting marks like that showed me that I could handle a career in architecture."

Often taken as a boy to the airport to watch planes, one student set his heart on becoming an airline pilot. There was agreement between parents and teachers that he should go on past high school, though counsellors wanted him to go to university and become an engineer. His parents agreed with his preference for college since he could take applied courses related to his goal. The mainstay was the unfailing support of his family.

The daughter of a company president was encouraged by her parents, teachers, and early employers to go as far as possible in school and at work. Her father said she could be whatever she wanted. She took a degree in science and worked in various departments of her father's business on the way to a management position. She was innovative, overcoming bias against women, and, through experience and by taking courses, learned every aspect of the business. For a while she was a machinist's helper, with dirty overalls and sweaty face.

Most upward strivers said they had worked hard in high school and since. Few, however, had a smooth transition to above-average jobs. Many tried other things before setting a firm goal. Individual behaviour and choice have an independent bearing on attainment.

The daughter of a couple with modest status aimed at becoming a lawyer but switched to the more difficult goal of medicine. "I haven't become a doctor yet, but all through high school I struggled to be a good student and daughter, to do the right thing. The subjects were not very hard, but some teachers made them hard to take. I worked because I had a goal, a lot of family support, and friends with similar objectives.

"By itself, school provided little motivation. We weren't taken seriously – especially girls. But I can see the light at the end of the tunnel. You have to work so hard. I'm looking forward to the job, the security and the feeling of having made it, since I'm the only one in our family to go on to higher education." In her case consonance between elders was weak; her own determination kept her on the path, along with the support of family and friends.

A test engineer had moderate support from his parents, who had only high school educations. But largely as a result of a co-op placement in electronics, he set his sights on engineering. His boss took him into the firm part time because he did well as a co-op student. What first attracted him to this field was a display in Grade Nine. His parents and teachers believed he should aim for a lower-level job than he wanted. In high school he wasn't sure of himself and didn't work hard. He went back to college because he was motivated after working for a while.

A worker in a home for emotionally disturbed seniors is also a volunteer at a young offenders' centre. Her goal is to be a probation officer and she is taking courses part time towards that end. Her parents are separated but her mother encourages her and sets an example. They are person-centred. She likes taking courses and she is confident of reaching her goal. There was little consonance between her family and other elders in setting goals for her; if there had been, she might have chosen a goal sooner.

Some innovators are self-employed. One thought during high school that she would become a chartered accountant, since she was good at maths. But there was little consonance in the aspirations of elders for her education and employment. She started dancing when she was four, took lessons, and began teaching dance as a classroom assistant. Now she owns a dance school and is always taking courses to improve her art.

The son of well-educated immigrants was not much interested in school; lacking clear direction, he left university before finishing. His father had taken him as a boy to see poverty-ridden areas at home before emigrating. "If you don't want to be poor, you must work hard." He worked in the family business during school term and in the summers. Then, with family backing, he formed a real estate agency. This meant taking course after course. The firm has grown and he has learned managerial skills.

Innovators by and large come from families where there are even chances of consensus between elders for their education and careers. While consensus helps, many innovators press on anyway, supported by their own ambition and commitment.

Conservatives

This is also the case for many who choose careers on the basis of convention. For these youth satisfaction comes not so much from challenge as from security.

A young accountant admitted that he is not greatly interested in his work; other things are just as important. His passion is flying and this is expensive. Working at courses that lead to a degree is not a burden because it provides security and a good income.

During high school one girl hoped to become a physiotherapist, but this meant years at university. Instead she set accounting as her goal and took basic courses at college. She will take training for advancement but is unhappy that promotion is slow in the civil service. Her decisions were rarely challenged by parents, teachers, or early employers.

A young man had a confusing time at school in the wake of his parents' divorce. His father had money but never supported him. His mother did her best but had little education. He feels that in high school there should be more emphasis on choosing a career. "Then kids would be motivated to take studies seriously. I drifted into office work and went to a business college for several terms. I'm paying off a student loan and can't afford more courses just now. But I hope to be a systems analyst. I'm a programmer now. It's a good job."

A data entry clerk has enough education (Grade Twelve) and job training to achieve security and moderate satisfaction at work. She hasn't the resources or interest to do more since she is the busy single parent of two small children. She was ostracized in Grade Thirteen during her first pregnancy. This caused extreme stress, disrupting her studies. Her parents provided strong support and helped all they could, despite their own modest education and jobs. But she received little help from teachers or early employers.

Sample youth who were not innovators or conservatives for the most part viewed employment from one of two angles. One group, 12 percent of the sample, rejected a career as top priority. They are non-careerists for one reason or another. The others, 15 percent of the sample, are at present uncommitted. Either they are uncertain about a career or they are in a tentative stage of choosing one. Some have returned to school with this in mind.

Non-Careerists

A young teacher is highly committed to helping students but not to a career. Other things are just as important. He was "clueless" about his own work plans in high school and during his first year at a large university. Then he went as a volunteer to a program for service by youth. "I went along with the crowd without considering options such as co-op and job training. I was expected to know what I wanted to do with my life. It wasn't until the youth program that I figured that out."

A fourth year university student plans to enter law school. He's willing but unenthusiastic about further training and thinks family, social life, and recreation are just as important as a career. Both his parents finished high school and hold skilled jobs. They supported him morally and financially; several teachers and a grandparent were also encouraging. There was consonance about his education but little vocational direction.

Uncommitted

A young mother who may go to college to prepare for health services is typical of entry-level workers who are uncertain of their futures. At present she is a waitress, supplementing her husband's income. Her co-op placement had been in a nursing home, which she found helpful, though she would have preferred to be in recreation. She finished Grade Twelve, but without enthusiasm. Her husband supports her goals but her parents were not helpful.

Most uncommitted youth work at low levels. A fork-lift operator and truck driver is satisfied, especially with the pay (over $700 a week). Sometimes he'd like to go back and become a skilled worker, but since he didn't get a diploma, it would take some doing. No one helped him with transition. Certainly there was no consonance in aspirations.

One non-conformist left school without a diploma to become a stuntman in movies and TV. He attended a special school but an accident ended his brief career. Since most of his courses had been in theatre and music, he now works part time as a drummer, disc jockey, or barkeeper. He loves his work and being broke doesn't worry him much. He didn't ask for help in transition since he knew what he wanted to do.

A woman specialist in the use of chemicals to grow lawns is not sure what she wants to do. She took post-secondary courses at two colleges but is still adrift. Her father was too pushy, but her mother helped in transition. Teachers and employers tried, but finally it was up to her. She could not decide. "I'll stay with my present job, even if chemicals are toxic, until I get bored. Then I'll move on." A shipper-receiver had 14 jobs in the six years since he dropped out of high school. He now wishes he had taken co-op and more counselling. His dad, a skilled tradesman, tried to help him but he couldn't decide on a goal.

CHAPTER EIGHT

Testing the Model: Transition as a Cumulative Process

Which are the most important forces that launch youth into productive, satisfying jobs? Following the holistic model outlined in chapter 1, we have seen that structural variables such as social class, gender, and ethnicity have a powerful impact on attainment. Yet youth themselves play the critical part in determining their future. By mid-adolescence they normally accept, reject, or modify the expectations of adults and peers (Anisef et al. 1980; Ashton and Lowe 1991; Ryrie 1983; Crysdale and MacKay 1994). Some who inherit privilege may learn behaviour that gives them a good start. But others drift into unproductive and ungratifying paths.

Family resources, cultural and financial, may extend the period of exploration but cannot by themselves ensure a smooth transition. Most young people, endowed with limited cultural and material capital, have a shorter time to flounder before social reality takes over. Most settle for modest gains and whatever security the work they find may provide. A disturbing minority, one-third in the mid-1980s, about one-fifth now, are denied or spurn the opportunities that further education and training may offer.

For most the die seems to be cast in mid-adolescence, when they are in Grades Ten or Eleven (Anisef et al. 1980). Some internalize the values of the dominant liberal middle class and strive in school towards job goals that are as high as or higher than those of their parents. Individual choice, ability, and effort are the catalysts that turn opportunity into achievement.

There is an ironic difference in ways parents and youth may see their roles. Almost one-half of the sample in their early 20s had moved away from home in the past two or three years, but the majority maintained active contacts with parents. Asked about how much influence the family had on their children's transition, only one-quarter of parents said that it had been strong. But youth had a much more favourable view, nearly two-thirds praising mothers for help and over one-half crediting fathers with support.

This chapter analyzes the process in two ways. First, we use multiple regression equations, step by step, to learn which background and intermediate variables had the most impact on outcomes. Then we use case studies to illustrate the patterns disclosed by statistical analysis.

THE SOURCES OF POSITIVE TRANSITION

The principal outcomes or dimensions of transition in our model are educational and occupational attainment, innovativeness in career planning, stable employment, pay, intrinsic satisfaction, and job training (see chapter 1, Figure 1–1).

Multiple regression allows us to single out the strongest antecedents of each dimension. As with all measures of association, there are limits to this method. While it winnows out weaker antecedents in successive equations, these carry with them part of the explanatory power of the equation. What is left, however, are the strongest antecedents of a particular outcome, calculated in terms of significance, or probability of happening by chance and not by sampling bias or error.

Virtually every study concludes that the most persistent antecedent of a positive passage from school to work is education.[1] We found in chapter 2 that parental aspirations for education depend partly on their social status, indicated by schooling and occupation.

However, the effects of background factors are indirect, operating through youth's marks and job plans, reinforced by help from peers (Table A–13). These are individual determinants. One structural variable – consonance in elders' educational and job aspirations for youth – affects educational attainment significantly, though not as strongly as individual factors. Success gathers momentum through high school, securing for some a positive launch into work. The model accounts for 36 percent of variance in education, a meaningful level.

Finer analysis helps us understand how education is achieved. First we ask what factors contribute most to the attainment of high marks. The equation on marks (not shown), demonstrates that, as with educational level, individual variables affect performance more than others' help or aspirations do. Effort makes the greatest difference in marks, followed by job expectation. Two normative factors are next: attendance at worship and the efficacy of belief. A structural background factor also helps – elders' overall aspirations.

Worship apparently strengthens hopes and focuses behaviour; belief that one can express values on the job is also associated significantly with high marks. This equation is reliable, explaining 31 percent of variance in marks.

Job expectations are boosted first by maternal occupation; women with high positions have a strong influence on their children's transition. Youth's education and marks come next, followed by the overall aspirations of elders for youth. The equation (not shown) is reliable, explaining 28 percent of variance in job expectations.

The second dimension of transition is *present job level.* Table A–14 shows which earlier factors are most likely to lead to higher-than-average jobs. This equation accounts for 27 percent of the variance. Again, both background and individual variables lead to job attainment. The strongest is job expectation ten years hence – an individual factor.

The second strongest source of present job level is closeness between school courses and present jobs – a structural factor. Again, only 26 percent of youth said that their schooling prepared them closely for their present job.

Maternal more than paternal occupation is significantly related with youth's present job status. This reflects the upward thrust of women's entrance into full-time work and rising expectations for their children. At present, sample women generally occupy lower levels or structures than men. Inequality of opportunity persists, but for the indomitable this may goad ambition and commitment.

Education and marks are not significantly related with present early jobs because of the prolonged blurring of education and employment among young adults in Canada (A.M. Thomas 1989; Ashton and Lowe 1991; cf. Rosenbaum and Kariya 1991; Krahn and Lowe 1991). Those with higher education are either just entering the market or studying. They must still acquire experience. Further education for some could alter the later work distribution. There is a general tendency, however, for entry jobs to predict long-term careers.

Innovativeness in career planning is a positive individual attribute in adaptation to the new job market. We consider youth who chose the following statement to be innovative: "I am working or soon will be in a field where there are new approaches, methods, and opportunities. These will require further training from time to time."

Table A–15 shows the strongest sources of innovativeness, beginning with present higher-than-average jobs. More than others, innovators also acknowledge unusual help from fathers and they are apt to be of non-Anglo, non-Franco origin (cf. Beiser 1994, Devoretz 1995). Further, youth who had taken school courses that were closely related to their present jobs were more apt to be innovative. While the equation is not strong, it is significant, explaining 20 percent of variance in innovativeness.

Another dimension of a smooth passage is *work stability*, or absence of unemployment. Virtually one-half the sample had been unemployed since leaving high school five years earlier, mostly once or twice. The average length of unemployment was slightly under three months. The strongest predictors of stable employment are shown in Table A–16.

The main antecedents of youth unemployment are background structures in which youth have little say: lack of democratic decision making at home, poorly educated fathers, and an absence of paternal help and of consonance between the hopes of elders. Another antecedent is low levels of education among youth themselves. The way a family reaches decisions affects a person's self-reliance; democratic process reduces the likelihood of unemployment.

That the model explains only 15.8 percent of variance in unemployment raises the possibility of alternative explanations. The most likely one is that unemployment among youth is so common that fine distinctions are tenuous. In spite of a growing economy, unemployment among 17- to 24-year-olds has mounted to 17 percent currently because of the decline in traditional entry-level jobs, the mismatch between education and work, the scarcity of training, and the pre-emption of positions by older, experienced

workers. This has happened despite a relative decline in the size
of the younger age group (cf. Marquardt 1996, 34).

Consideration of *present pay* as an indicator of adjustment to
work also raises questions. Some young workers with secondary
schooling or less have more experience and better pay than others who have more education. Their advantage evaporates, however, after a few years once graduates of colleges and universities
have been in the labour force long enough to win better positions.

Only two antecedents contribute significantly to the equation
on pay at this time – rank of position and being a woman. Together they account for 25.6 percent of the variance in pay (Table
A–17).

Regardless of qualifications, women are kept at lower levels and
earn less than men. This is a stubborn structural hurdle that only
public opinion and legislation can dismantle. Meanwhile, it dis-
torts what otherwise would be a more rational and just pay scale.

Youth income has decreased both absolutely and relatively
since the 1980s. Between 1981 and 1992 the real income of men
aged 17 to 24, for example, fell by over 18 percent (ibid.). This is
further evidence of the vulnerability of the young in today's labour market.

Intrinsic satisfaction logically should be a good indicator of positive transition. But education, marks, and job expectation could
explain only 14 percent of variance in inner satisfaction – a positive but weak equation. Other significant factors are maternal education and gender equality norms.

The weakness of this equation may be explained partly by general satisfaction among young workers. Most savour their new independence as they appropriate some rewards of adulthood –
their own quarters, a car, a family, and a few luxuries. Many, however, confuse the euphoria of new status with intrinsic career satisfaction. The worth of a useful and gratifying job in itself may be
realized only when the novelty of independence has worn off.

Finally, in a technologized, competitive market the launch into
work might logically be accompanied by *on-the-job training*. But our
best equation accounts for only six percent of variance in such
training. The only predictor that approaches significance is gender. Women systematically have fewer opportunities for training
on the job than men. Education, job level, expectations, effort,

and background make no difference. An insufficient number of job entrants receive enough training to produce a more meaningful explanation.

CAMEOS OF TRANSITION

We have shown that three-quarters of the youth sample are committed to either an innovative or a conservative career. The other quarter are uncommitted or not seriously interested in a career. Most of the latter are willing to work but only as a means to other ends – recreation and homemaking, for example.

The following case studies illustrate how youth enter the work market. Each case is reported rather fully, avoiding snippets of information. These are cameos of real people. To preserve anonymity, some details are scrambled.

High Achievers

The strong influence of mothers is clearly illustrated in the case of Erik, whose mother was born in Norway. His father left the family when Erik was very young. "Mother is the most important person in my life. She supports me in all my endeavours. She has inspired me to work hard, although I could have tried harder in high school. A couple of friends were also very helpful, and I'm strongly self-motivated."

Erik's parents never went past high school but he was determined to go further. His chief interests were science and maths, and his early career goal was to be a research scientist. He graduated in engineering and plans now to set up a consulting business.

Erik scores high in dimensions of positive transition: education, marks and effort at school, job entry level, pay, job training, intrinsic satisfaction, and innovative career planning. "The main purpose of education should be to communicate well in society and culture. Next it should teach life skills. The actual purpose in schools is to get you through with good marks, although a few teachers take a personal interest in students."

He usually practises his beliefs, taught to him by his mother, which are based on religious faith. He is a regular church-goer. The three cardinal virtues for him are honesty, integrity and loyalty.

Norman, another achiever, feels that his close-knit family influenced his transition quite strongly, though they didn't urge a career on him. "But Mom was always pushing me at school. I'd come home with 85 percent and she'd say, 'Why not 90?' She provided strong motivation and self-reliance. 'Do it yourself' she'd say, and I would. Dad was my advisor; he helped me choose a career and try it out. His military training got through to me. I learned inner discipline from him. A friend who's a teacher helped me develop a balance. He said, 'It's okay to have a social life as well as a work life.'

"My girl friend also helped me get turned outward. I didn't need help from teachers and counsellors as much as other kids, I guess. Some peers reinforce my goals. They're there for the same reasons I am – they want to get ahead and they like the work. I help younger students and that makes accounting clearer to me as well. But it all started at home."

Sandy had been a school dropout; his goals clashed with those of his parents. From Grade Ten on he wanted to be a musician. "Music is my passion and dream." Now he's back at school and hopes to take music at university. His mother helped with homework, checked timetables, and discussed ideas and theories. Sandy's worst subject was maths, but his teacher cared about him. Once he grasped the procedures he never forgot them. His best friend also helped him get on his feet and finally pass Grade Twelve. He is hyperactive and finds it hard to sit through class. After he dropped out, he got into music seriously and that changed his views on education. "Before starting full-time work, I want to get as much schooling as I can – musically, psychologically, philosophically, and socially. When you explore the world with its poverty, misery, and yearning, you realize what education could do for others as well as yourself.

"My parents and I clashed chiefly because they urged on me their goal of security through a conventional job. My view of education is different; it's about how theories connect separate ideas and facts, to socialize us into living in peace, to teach values that will bring everyone in the world together. I'd like to be a musician so that creativity will lead to a better life for all, as well as for me."

Sandy could be labelled a dreamer, yet his strong commitment reflects innovativeness.

Sometimes youth are determined to enter a career in spite of weak parental support. Audrey's people were of little help, though they set standards for her. Each had a good education, the father a BA and the mother a nurse's training. Audrey left school after completing a diploma course but is not working now since she is caring for her first child. She and her husband share responsibilities. Her firm goal is to become a psychologist, partly because of her own experience. As a student she suffered from dyslexia; a school counsellor helped her recover. Now she wants to understand behaviour to better cope with life and help others. Moreover, she is determined to get a degree since her parents put aside savings for her brother's university education but not for hers.

Virginia's parents were divorced when she was three. She lived with her mother, whose education led only to low-paying jobs. She lacked the resources to help Virginia move up. "My father expected me to be a homemaker. The most helpful person was an English teacher, although good friends were also encouraging. The teacher said I should go to university and become a writer."

Virginia is now a university psychology major and works part time as a receptionist. While a daycare helper, she saw the needs of children and decided to become a social worker.

Malcolm is an innovator in spite of the absence of parental support. His ambition to become an actor was disapproved of by his people and that led to severe emotional stress. But he persisted and gradually took control of his life, with the help of a school counsellor. Peers in drama provided the strongest support. He took part-time work as a freelance film animator. The artistic possibilities fascinated him. Now, in addition to his job, he attends college to improve his skills. Malcolm criticizes schools, perhaps paradoxically.

"They overemphasize teaching skills to the detriment of the individual. More attention should be paid to the traumatic emotional and social changes students experience. Emotional stress often sadly diverts attention from future plans, including advanced education and careers."

Malcolm recognizes the tensions that accompany the spread of technologies. "I need the computer when doing film animation, but it reduces the imaginative skills the artist should bring to the process. Disneyesque skills are being lost and we are left with the

Smurfs and other Saturday morning crap. The computer cannot match the élan, grace, and detail of the human mind, eye, and hand."

While these cases demonstrate the determination of some socially diminished youth to enter innovative careers, they are exceptions. Usually, strong support by parents and educators is needed to launch a promising and productive career.

Mid-Level Strivers

Tony is a carpenter and loves it. His father is a tailor, as his grandfather was in the old country, and his mother is a dressmaker, also like her mother. Both get satisfaction from customers' appreciation. When Tony was in Grade Ten his parents hoped he would go to university and become a lawyer, but he didn't like school and didn't study. He misbehaved and was suspended, then worked for a while as a labourer, which he hated. His family never lost faith in him.

"They cared for me even when I was kicked out and coaxed me to go back and get the Grade Twelve diploma. Then my uncle taught me the trade and I became a skilled carpenter. Someday I hope to be a construction superintendent. I had trouble with English but loved maths. One teacher in the final year made me feel good about myself; the rest weren't much help. No one really helped me except the family and myself."

Uncommitted

In spite of parental encouragement, many young people do not take advantage of opportunities. Nancy's parents hoped that she would go to university but didn't say much to her about careers. Her father is a technician; her mother never had a full-time job outside the home. They say that their influence on her transition was "zilch."

Yet, though unskilled, unemployed, in debt, and discouraged, Nancy says that her parents had always been helpful. "They spend endless time encouraging me and providing support. I have good intentions but tend to procrastinate. I quit school in Grade Eleven because I was frustrated and didn't see that what I was doing would help me later. I did go back and got my diploma, but studying was boring and meaningless for me. If I'd known about co-op education it might have helped."

Nancy has worked for five years as a nurses' aide and really likes it, though conditions are not good. At present she's not committed to a career. In separate interviews, Nancy's mother approved of co-op, but her father said, "It's a waste of time. We should have more opportunities for apprenticeships. In theory co-op is good, but I don't see how it can be improved without more help from enlightened employers. Our youngest son is in it, but it needs tightening up, with better counselling and more coordination between school and workplace.

"The purpose of education should be dual: to prepare for life beyond school, and to round youth out, exposing them to knowledge over a wide range. You never know what spark of an idea might fire them up."

Parents in similar circumstances can have different impacts on their children's transition, often depending on the youth's responses and choices. Some youth with promising backgrounds have a negative passage from school to work. Brian didn't like school and left without a diploma. He let his parents down; they had hoped he would graduate and perhaps become an engineer or manager. His parents are professionals with degrees and say they tried to help. But he gives them little credit. His teachers didn't seem to care, although a counsellor encouraged him when he decided on trade school. He became an apprentice and is now first cook in a large hotel. He is dissatisfied with the job and wonders what he should be doing.

Students drop out for different reasons. Susan quit because she was pregnant and needed money. She never had any clear goals and works as a cashier in a grocery chain to support herself and her child. She never knew her father and says that her mother never helped. She hasn't time to make any friends. She'd like to become a secretary but has no plans to take courses. Yet this was not her choice. Friends, family, and school all failed her.

Entry to the working world was excessively rough for close to half of the youth in our sample. Structural restrictions deny what a democratic society promises – a fair chance to contribute and to enjoy the fruit of one's labour. Transition for the poor, many women, and most visible minorities, regardless of ambition and effort, is often blocked. Levelling the playing field by reforming structures would maximize personal initiative, a strong factor in launching a career.

CHAPTER NINE

Comparative Models of Transition: Canada, Britain, and Sweden

In its report on lifelong learning the OECD compares the proportion of 17-year-olds in member countries who were enrolled at school in 1992. This is a clue as to the ability of countries to retain students beyond the legal leaving age of 16, affecting the potential for entrants into the new labour market. In Canada and the US the proportion of 17-year-olds in school was much less than the 80 percent reported for the UK (including part-timers) and 87 percent for Sweden (OECD 1996B, 127).

In Canada and the United States there are examples of effective programs to improve youth's opportunities but most are left to chance, market forces, and their own devices to find the way. Youth are most successful in transition in countries where the parts played by the main actors in the labour market are closely integrated. These are educators, employers, workers, and the state. Because basic values and constitutional systems in Britain and Sweden are similar to those in Canada, we examine their provisions for transition with the thought that features of their systems may be adopted here.

Changes in Britain and Sweden, along with other countries caught up in the information era, are emerging around four principles: 1) curricula should integrate academic and vocational studies; 2) performance standards in education and occupations should be related; 3) basic education and training should include some work-based learning; and 4) educators and employers should share responsibility and power in school-to-work programming.

The new systems challenge and encourage students who were formerly thought to be less capable of advanced education and also attract youth whose background and aspirations are at high levels (Stern et al. 1997).

Britain has taken decisive steps to improve youth's passage through centralized public plans, in which educators and employers play key roles. In this chapter David Ashton describes training programs that clear the hurdle of traditional education in the UK and compares their assumptions and model with those in Canada. Rune Axelsson and Erik Wallin describe the long process of consultation and experiment in Sweden since World War II to integrate education and employment. In this process, teachers, parents, employers, and the state worked out generally acceptable measures. Older students participated. The underlying goal in Sweden is to reflect basic equalitarian values within a carefully defined labour market.

Our look at Britain and Sweden is prefaced with a brief review of Canadian efforts to improve relations between education and the labour market, with a reference to the United States.

CANADIAN INITIATIVES

Early in the 1990s the federal Employment and Immigration ministry introduced initiatives to help stem the leakage of youth from school. The Challenge Program was extended and the focus placed on secondary more than post-secondary students. Employers were subsidized to engage students for the summer. Work Orientation Workshops were expanded, helping potential and recent high school dropouts with counselling and practical experience. In most provinces, loans are available for students to create small businesses. Employment centres help youth find positions.

In the late 1980s the federal government undertook three initiatives. One expanded support for school programs – notably cooperative education, workshops, career week, and counselling. A second mobilized business, labour, the provinces, and others in developing solutions to the dropout problem. Finally, a national information campaign raised public awareness with the hope of encouraging youth to continue schooling. They allocated $296,000,000 over five years for these initiatives.

There is little sign, however, that Ottawa is forging longstanding policies and programs to deal with the education/training malaise. This may be the result of the jurisdictionary allocation of education to provinces and job training to federal authority. Consideration is now being given to devolution of training to provinces. Studies to overhaul transitional frameworks have been conducted in British Columbia, Alberta, Saskatchewan, Newfoundland, Ontario, and other provinces.

The major changes introduced into Alberta's school system to improve transition were discussed in chapter 5.

British Columbia, meanwhile, proclaimed a new School Act in 1989 that adopted many of the recommendations of the Sullivan Commission. Since then, a draft has been circulated for public discussion. *Year 2000: A Framework for Learning* (1990) elaborates policies and programs to bring education into the mainstream of modern technologized society.

After 11 years of primary and intermediate schooling, extending a common but flexible curriculum to all students, there will be two years of a "graduation program." The intermediate program is based on four principal strands: humanities, sciences, fine arts, and practical arts. All students are required to take courses in each strand and teachers are expected to take a holistic approach within courses. Career exploration is to be included. In the graduation years three directions are to be followed: intellectual development, human and social development, and career development. The latter includes options that lead to post-secondary choices: exploration, passport to apprenticeship, career preparation, community/school partnership, and university. The result, ideally, will be a much closer relationship between schools and the community, including families, employers, and public/private associations. Over 20,000 BC secondary students are now involved in some form of work experience or work study.

In Ontario the first Premier's Council report (1988) examined the province's competitive position vis-à-vis other major industrial countries. Ontario was found to be at a serious disadvantage in terms of research and development, particularly in the private sector, the preparation of students, teachers, and industrial leaders in science and technology, and upgrading student performance in mathematics and science.

The second Premier's Council report was entitled *People and Skills in the New Global Economy* (1990). In addition to making recommendations on higher education, training in industry and business, and standardizing subject credentials, the report focused on secondary school students, teaching, and relations with employers and communities. It was recommended that technical and career education should be improved and promoted, with employer involvement; that a common, destreamed curriculum for Grades Seven to Ten should be phased in by the year 2000; and that wider options should be available for credit at the upper secondary level. It is envisioned that some students will leave for employment, some will remain part-time at school and at school-related employment, and others will continue into post-secondary education, preferably linked with work experience.

Cooperative education is to be expanded and consideration given to pay for student workers; this would reduce the attraction of part-time work at low wages, usually unrelated to education, training, or careers. Incorporation of apprenticeships with co-op education would speed up and raise the quality of transition, providing students with more meaningful work and better pay than most part-time jobs now offer. The details for reform, as outlined in *Ontario Secondary Schools* (Ontario, Ministry of Education 1996), were discussed in chapter 4.

THE UNITED STATES

The drift in transition has received high level attention in the United States. Numerous ventures to address the issue have been started but as yet in many states little public action has been taken to change basic structures. A critical report on the renewal of the workforce was prepared for the Congressional Joint Economic Committee by the General Accounting Office in 1990. Entitled *Training Strategies: Preparing Non-college Youth for Employment in the US and Foreign Countries*, it disclosed the disadvantages of American youth compared with those in Japan, Sweden, West Germany, and the United Kingdom. It places responsibility for remedial action on educators and employers.

US international competitiveness is being eroded because most youth are unprepared to meet the need for technical skills. While the US is unequalled in the proportion of youth going to university, those not at college or university are ill equipped for work. At least nine million, or 27 percent, of the 33 million Americans who are between the ages of 16 and 24 are not learning the skills required to meet employment needs. Standards in literacy and numeracy are inferior, students are left on their own to find jobs, mostly without opportunity for upgrading, and, if out of work, they receive only a fraction of the training and help needed to become employable, compared with youth in competing nations.

The report recommends that *all* students attain the academic or technical skills necessary to perform effectively in post-secondary education or the workplace and that early assistance be provided to make this possible. There should be more school/work linkages such as apprentice-type and co-op education programs. The federal Departments of Education and Labour should assist state and local officials in the delivery of these services.

Disadvantaged minorities such as Hispanics and blacks require particular attention. US expenditures per capita for primary and secondary education are relatively less than in the four other countries in the study. Funding for US schooling comes primarily from state and local taxes and varies widely, depending on area economies. Most schools do little to link education with work; only three percent of American high school youth are reached through programs such as co-op education. Moreover, less than one-quarter of the children who need the help offered by Head Start and similar enriching programs are actually served.

Programs such as the Boston Compact, which links schools and employers, are exemplary but relatively scarce. In this program businesses agree to employ a quota of students at entry levels upon graduation from secondary programs in technical and commercial courses at schools in low-income areas. Technical secondary centres in wealthier states are of high quality but they are deficient in poorer states.

Other influential studies and commissions are critical and suggest similar remedies. These include the National Commission on the Reform of Secondary Education (1973), Coleman's report to the President's Science Advisory Committee (1974), the William T. Grant Foundation (1988), the W.E. Upjohn Institute for Employment Research (Levitan 1988) and numerous federal, state, and private sources (Rosenbaum 1996; Wells and Oakes 1996; Wenglinsky 1997). The 1994 School to Work Opportunities Act encourages states to keep four-year colleges open for every student to widen career choices. Whether the United States, like Canada, will have the political will to follow these challenges remains to be seen.

The 1990 report on training strategies notes that England and Sweden guarantee further education, skill training, or placement in a job for most unemployed youth. The programs are usually comprehensive and long term. England operates the Youth Training Scheme and Employment Training for out-of-school youth aged 16 and 17. The former provides two years of work experience and on-the-job training for 16-year-olds and one year for 17-year-olds. It also offers classes in Colleges of Further Education and pays a weekly stipend. Seventy percent of unemployed youth enrol, and it has been determined that three months after leaving, 80 percent of participants either had a job, were in training, or had embarked on further education. However, the opinion is widespread in the UK that these programs need upgrading and greater flexibility.

The US report says that Sweden guarantees employment and training for all jobless teenagers. Until age 18 these programs are administered by municipal authorities and after that by the national employment service. Those who cannot find work and do not want more schooling are offered public or private "induction" employment for six months, which pays less than market wages. They work four days a week and attend classes on the fifth. For 18- and 19-year-olds an individual plan is offered. Youth over 19 are included in adult programs, with vocational workshops, education, and services. They may also receive temporary public jobs, for which grants are paid.

TRANSITION IN BRITAIN[*][1]
DAVID N. ASHTON

Britain, like Canada, faces pressures for change that stem from intensified international competition in global markets and the impact of new technology. The resulting economic adjustments have been similar to those occurring in Canada, namely the decline of semi-skilled and unskilled jobs in the manufacturing sector and growth in professional, managerial, and scientific jobs and in part-

---

[*] Throughout this section, our study is referred to as "the Canadian Study."

time service sector jobs (Ashton et al. 1990). However, recent studies demonstrate that differences in institutional arrangements and in class structures and values have meant that the experience of transition is very different in the two societies (Ashton and Lowe 1991). As a result, interventions by government and official agencies, particularly those designed to create integration between education and productive work, have taken different forms. Knowledge of these differences is essential if we are to understand and evaluate the part played in transition by policy innovations such as the cooperative education programs in Canada.

Differences in Institutional Structures

The British educational system is highly centralized and highly stratified. Unlike Canada, where education is under provincial jurisdiction and subject to local control, the central government in Britain is the major source of funds for, and traditionally has imposed specific forms of educational organization on, the local authorities who deliver the service. Immediately after the Second World War this led to the provision of grammar schools for the academically able, the top ten or fifteen percent (predominantly from the middle class), and a few technical schools for able but practical working-class youth destined for manual labour.

During the 1960s the central government progressively replaced these with comprehensive schools, but within such schools the division between the academically able who were capable of success in public examinations and the remainder was perpetuated by a system of streaming. In this process there was no room for parental involvement. Only in Scotland was central control more distanced, with broadly similar forms of delivery but with control centred in the Scottish Office (Gray et al. 1983) and a separate system of Scottish public examinations. In essence the form of educational provision and the broad structure of the curriculum was imposed *centrally* with different types of provision for the various classes and status groups.

The training system in Britain is also very different from that in Canada. Whereas Canadian firms have traditionally relied on immigrants to provide a pool of trained labour, British employers and trade unions have adopted elements of the mediaeval apprenticeship system to provide the basis for a system of training for those, usually males, destined for skilled manual jobs in manufacturing. Young people are recruited for such training while still at school or immediately on leaving (currently at age 16), and not, as in Canada, after completion of a probationary period within the firm. The system of work training in Britain has therefore always been more closely articulated to the educational system than in Canada.

The other distinctive feature of the British system of training has been the existence since the 1960s of strong central government input. This has taken a number of different forms under various governments, ranging from attempts to impose industry-wide standards through training boards to the attempt to establish a comprehensive national system of training for all groups by the former Manpower Services Commission. However, like educational provision, training provision has traditionally been characterized by an attempt by the central government to impose uniform national schemes on different localities and industries.

The point of similarity between the two societies lies in the provision of training for women. This is concentrated in the educational system, with training for clerical work, business, computing, and low-level service occupations taking place in some schools but primarily in Colleges of Further Education.

These institutional structures reflect the distinctive values and class structure of British society. In Britain, ideas such as equality of opportunity have always been subordinated to considerations of deference and "knowing one's place." Hence the concern in Britain has been to tailor the education and training of each status group for its future position in the system of stratification and division of labour. This contrasts markedly with the Canadian belief in egalitarianism and forms of provision that maximize equality of opportunity and individual responsibility for determining the route taken through the system.

The relationship between educational and training institutions in Britain has created a series of clearly identifiable and highly structured pathways through the educational system and into the labour market. The research literature enables us to identify three such pathways, each of which has associated with it a distinctive set of orientations required by those who follow the route (Ashton and Field 1976; Jenkins 1983; P. Brown 1987). The first pathway at the base of the system is a route through the lower streams of the schools from which young people emerge without qualifications into unskilled and semi-skilled jobs. Their orientation to school has been characterized as one of rejection, which in some instances involves the inversion of the values of the school. For these young people the school has nothing to offer.

The second pathway is through the middle streams of the comprehensive school and into skilled manual and low-level clerical jobs. This stream is followed by what the literature refers to as ordinary working-class kids (P. Brown 1987). They accept the necessity of schooling as a means of acquiring the credentials that are believed necessary for entry into an apprenticeship or the equivalent. Beyond that they have no commitment to school or education.

Finally, at the apex of the state education system are those, usually from middle-class and "aspiring" working-class origins, who follow the third pathway and move through the higher streams, perform well in public examinations, and continue their education beyond age 16 in preparation for entry into the professions, management, and administration.

This system endured throughout the 1960s and 1970s and gave transition in Britain some of its enduring features. Foremost among these is early leaving. Whereas in Canada about 20 percent drop out of school before completing their education, usually around age 18, in Britain the majority leave school at 16; indeed, in 1988 only 39 percent of 16- and 17-year-olds remained in full-time education. Moreover, once having left school these young people will not return. Their attitudes towards education are such that they can no longer see any relevance in it, given their position in the labour market. At best education is seen as irrelevant (Willis 1977; P. Brown 1987). This contrasts markedly with the findings of research on Canadian youth (Krahn and Lowe 1991; Krahn 1991), for whom transition is characterized by constant movement to and fro between education and work until such time as the young person settles down in the labour market. This is associated with a widespread acceptance of the importance of education and a continued belief in its efficacy, even amongst those who have dropped out (Tanner 1991).

One other distinctive feature of the relationship between the educational system, labour market, and training institutions in Britain is the existence of a formal agency, the Careers Service.

Funded by the central government, the service is responsible for advising school leavers about careers and helping to place them in a job. It is charged with the task of interviewing and advising every school leaver.

Recent Changes in Structuring Transition

During the last decade we have witnessed at least three different sets of changes that affect the structuring of transition in Britain. The first, initiated in the mid-1970s by a Labour government under the title "The Great Debate," comprised an attempt to explore ways of bringing together education and industry. At the local level, one consequence of that dialogue was the attempt by a number of schools to introduce work experience. This was done along the lines of a similar program in Canada, with young people being given the opportunity to work for a short period, usually less than four weeks, in a local organization. Some local authorities also introduced a related program of teacher secondment to industry, aimed at providing teachers with greater insight into industrial conditions. While many schools now have established work experience programs, these are primarily directed at lower-ability pupils, while the teachers and parents of pupils in the higher streams tend to see such activities as "interfering" with academic work.

Another related development has been the gradual extension of careers education courses, which include instruction on available occupations, methods of job search, and life and social skills. However, they are non-examination subjects and their introduction has been somewhat haphazard; some schools operate without them.

The second set of changes came as a consequence of the 1979–82 recession. This was far more severe in Britain than in Canada, the estimated rates of unemployment for 16-year-olds reaching 49.8 percent in January 1982 and 68 percent in January 1984, while the rates for 16- to 18-year-olds were 32.7 and 39.1 percent (Raffe 1987).

These rates concealed tremendous regional variations. While the labour market remained relatively buoyant in areas of London and the Southeast, it virtually collapsed in parts of the Midlands, northern England, and Scotland, with few school leavers finding jobs. Associated with the growth of mass youth unemployment was the demise of the apprenticeship system as 20 percent of manufacturing capacity was lost and the remaining firms cut back on training. In 1979 the total number of apprentices in Great Britain was 155,000; by 1985 this had fallen to 73,200. This ruptured the pathways into the labour market, especially those leading to manual occupations.

The government responded by introducing the Youth Training Scheme (YTS), which was to provide a year's (later two years') full-time training and work experience for every school leaver who could not find a job. The government deliberately implemented the scheme through employers rather than through the education system in an attempt to reduce the power of local authorities and make YTS responsive to market needs. It involved a minimum of 13 weeks off-the-job training, but most of the time was devoted to work experience. Entrants were paid a weekly trainee allowance rather than a wage. In 1982, its first year of operation, YTS catered to 354,000 entrants (Ashton et al. 1989), although the quality of the schemes varied considerably, some serving as the first year of an apprenticeship and others providing little more than free labour for employers who gave little or no training in return (Lee et al. 1990). In 1989 attendance was made virtually compulsory as the government withdrew welfare or social security assistance from those who refused a YTS placement.

A third set of changes was aimed at transforming the educational system. Essentially these changes reintroduced forms of stratification similar to those that characterized the tripartite system introduced after the Second World War. They included the Technical Vocational Education Initiative (TVEI). Schools whose income from the central government had been cut were offered extra funds through the Manpower Services Commission for introducing a more vocationally oriented curriculum. Although originally intended for pupils of all levels of ability, in effect the new curriculum was directed at working-class pupils in the lower streams of the educational system. In response partly to the changes introduced by TVEI and partly to the demands of a minority of working-class pupils who remained in education after failing to obtain a job, various other vocational qualifications and programs were also introduced.

In addition, part of the funding of the Further Education Colleges that traditionally provided vocational education for those over 16 (for example, the theoretical instruction required for apprentices) was shifted from the control of the Local Authority to the centralized, employment-led Manpower Services Commission, to make further education more responsive to market needs.

A further component of education reforms was the introduction of City Technology Colleges, a small number of colleges, largely financed by industry, whose aim was to provide high-quality technical education. In addition, state comprehensive schools were encouraged to opt out of Local Authority control and receive their funding direct from the state. The result of these measures has been to introduce a new form of selectivity into the state system.

The latest educational reform has been the introduction of a centrally controlled national curriculum that is to be mandatory in all state schools. However, this curriculum is to be primarily academic in character and is likely to undermine the vocationally oriented TVEI. To a certain extent, Scotland, with its own educational system and its own system of vocational education, SCOTVEC, has been shielded from some of these changes, which are confined to England and Wales (Raffe and Courtenay 1988).

New Routes through the System

The result of these changes has been to differentiate further between the three pathways into the labour market depicted in Figure 9–1. The first pathway has become differentiated into routes 1 and 2. Route 1 is taken by those with few or no educational qualifications who leave school and succeed in entering a full-time job. This route is far more common in the southeast of England; for example, Bynner (1991) found that in 1985, in the affluent town of Swindon, 32 percent of 16-year-olds had left school and entered a job, compared with 9 percent in depressed Liverpool. Many of these young people will experience spells of unemployment.

Route 2 is taken by the unqualified who enter the Youth Training Scheme. Of the 1985 cohort, YTS accounted for 18 percent of those in Swindon and 34 percent of those in Liverpool. Many of these young adults will experience spells of unemployment as well as periods of employment in semi-skilled or unskilled jobs (Ashton and Maguire 1986; Roberts et al. 1986).

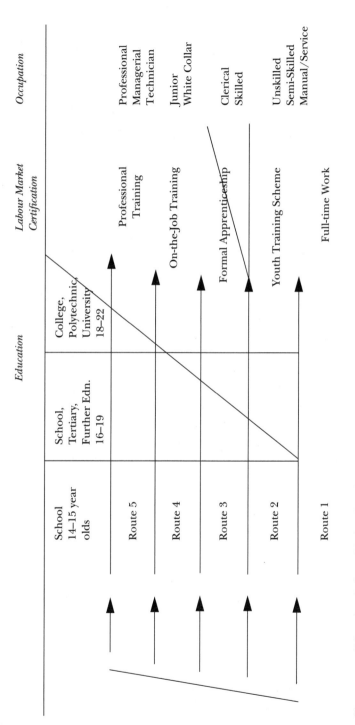

Figure 9–1   Education, Labour Market Certification, and Occupation in Britain

The third route is taken by those who usually attain an "accept-able" level of performance in the public examinations (GCSE) at 16 and then leave for an apprenticeship.

Route four is followed by those who also achieve a minimal level of certification in the exams at 16 and who then continue in the comprehensive school or enter a College of Further Education for vocational training before entering white collar work. The fifth route is the traditional academic route, which involves stay-ing on at school until age 18 and then entering a university or polytechnic.

Experiences in Transition

The routes depicted in Figure 9–1 inevitably involve an element of oversimplification. However, the fact that they are identifiable and that research has revealed clear differences in the orienta-tions of young people who follow them highlights some of the consequences of the more highly structured transition that is so characteristic of British society when compared with Canada. Without an understanding of these differences, attempts to com-pare results from studies in the two societies can lead to mislead-ing conclusions. With these differences in societal context in mind that we turn to a comparison of the findings from *this* study of Canadian youth's experience of the transition to work with the findings of similar studies in the UK.

The more highly stratified system of education in Britain and the clearly articulated links between the routes through the edu-cational system and the labour market mean that all pupils after age 13, parents, and teachers have fairly clear and "realistic" ideas about likely educational achievements and occupational destinations of youth. Under the tripartite system, young people were selected for the different types of school at age 11; they would then have a clear idea about their likely destination in the labour market. Since then, the introduction of comprehensives has meant that the process has been delayed a little, but by age 13 or 14 most pupils are aware of their likely fate in the public examinations and hence their likely position in the labour mar-ket (West 1983).

Thus, the Canadian findings that over one-half of students ex-pressed the parental hope that they would go to university, and that 50 percent hope to be managers, are unlikely to be found in a comparable British study. By the time the young person is 13 or 14, all the parties concerned will be aware that the majority of young people will have left the educational system by age 16. Moreover, once they leave very few return to education, even when no jobs are available (Bynner 1991). Only those following the "academic" route can "realistically" aspire to university education.

Similarly, a number of studies have found that the majority of young working-class pupils and their parents regard a skilled manual occupation (for males) and clerical/secretarial work (for females) as their occupational goal (Griffin 1985; P. Brown 1987; Cockburn 1987; Furlong 1987). It is only among those from middle-class backgrounds and those following route 5 that a majority would aspire to professional, managerial, or technical occupation.

Another difference is the significance of marks. In Britain these are of far less significance than in Canada; what is critical is not the marks awarded at school but the number of passes obtained in the public examinations taken at 16. This exam denotes the end of compulsory schooling and the success or otherwise of the young people taking it determines which avenues or routes will be open to them in the future. However, success in these examinations is closely linked to the parents' occupational status and educational achievements (Gray et al. 1983).

In terms of outcomes, young people in Britain, like their Canadian counterparts, look to such factors as the level of income, interest, and conditions of work for the main source of their rewards. However, British findings suggest that intrinsic rewards such as interesting work become less significant, while extrinsic rewards, especially money, become more important as young people mature in years and take on family commitments (Ashton and Maguire 1986).

The amount of training a young person receives varies in accordance with whether or not the job offers a formal traineeship or apprenticeship. If the latter is the case then the training may last up to five years. In 1975 35 percent of males had received apprenticeship training compared to 5 percent of females (National Child Development Study 1981). For those entering semi-skilled and unskilled jobs the majority receive less than one month's training (Ashton et al. 1990).

The other point of contrast when comparing outcomes in the two societies concerns the role of structural factors. British studies (Ashton and Maguire 1986; Roberts et al. 1986; Furlong 1987; Bynner 1991) all point to greater awareness among young adults of the role of economic conditions and other structural factors in determining whether or not they will be successful in acquiring any job at all, never mind one that approximates their own aspirations.

Thus, both the national level of unemployment and local economic conditions are powerful factors in determining the outcome of transition in the UK. And while young people there nevertheless tend to underplay the significance of these external conditions in determining their own fortunes, they are made forcefully aware of them when seeking jobs. Studies in the mid-1980s showed the most common reason for accepting a job was that it was the only one available (Ashton and Maguire 1986; Roberts et al. 1986).

Overall, when focusing on the experiential dimension of transition, one of the strongest contrasts that emerges between British and Canadian findings is the degree to which Canadian youth take on responsibility for negotiating the transition themselves. This comes through very clearly in the case studies presented in earlier chapters. Although parents and teachers may influence them, young Canadians tend to make their own decisions. Counsellors are there to provide advice and teachers provide opportunities and support, but the final decisions tend to be seen as the responsibility of the young person concerned. In Britain parents are also seen as the most important source of advice, followed by teachers and the careers officer. But precisely because they are in more highly structured pathways and routes, there is less scope for individual choice. Within the different routes, all parties concerned know what the realistic options are. Students who fail the public examination at 16 are aware that their options are restricted to semi-skilled and unskilled manual and service sector work.

A large part of the careers officer role, in contrast to that of the Canadian school counsellor, is to "cool out" those who are about to leave school with unrealistic aspirations. The only caveat to be introduced here concerns the methodology employed in the Canadian study and comparable British ones. Work by the Labour Market Studies Group at the University of Leicester suggests that, if asked who was most influential in their decision making, a high proportion of school leavers would reply parents and teachers. However, the further away they are from the point of decision (in terms of age), the greater the propensity to attribute significance for the decision to themselves.

With regard to the gender issue, the situation in Britain is similar in some respects to that revealed elsewhere in this study. In Britain young females have recently outperformed young males in the public examinations (GCSE) taken by 16-year-olds, but males catch up by age 18 and perform better than females in universities. Also, by age 18 and beyond, males have a higher participation rate in further and higher education (Dex 1988).

In this respect, Canada has gone much further along the road to gender equality. Teachers' expectations of 16-year-old females, both in terms of examination success and occupational placement, are higher than for males (Furlong 1987). But in spite of their better educational performance, 16- and 17-year-old females finish up in lower-paid jobs. A higher proportion of females than males stay on in education after they reach 16, primarily to secure vocational qualifications and training in the field of clerical and service sector work. Yet once in work they receive less training than males. This is partly because females are largely excluded from apprenticeships. With regard to the commitment of young women to work, findings in the two societies are the same: they have as strong a commitment to participation in the labour market and look for rewards similar to those of their male counterparts (Griffin 1985; Wallace 1987).

In Britain, the significance of mothers and fathers in the decision-making process of young people has been well established. In general the findings are that mothers have more influence on their daughters' decision making and fathers on their sons' (Griffin 1985; Breakwell and Weinberger 1986; Wallace 1987; Furlong 1987). However, unlike the situation revealed in the Canadian study, there is no evidence that mothers are more influential overall. This factor may not have been effectively measured in Britain, or it may be that the women's movement and women in general have made greater gains in Canada than in Britain. I suspect that the latter is the case. It is significant in this respect that British studies have rarely, if ever, sought to measure beliefs about gender equality.

The impact of ethnicity on school performance and labour market participation has some similarities in the two societies. The great majority of young have received all their education in Britain. Of that group, most British-born Asian children do well at school relative to white children while their Afro-Caribbean counterparts do less well (Jenkins 1983). Yet once in the labour market, both groups are at a disadvantage in relation to whites (Lee and Wrench 1983). Thus, while most young Asians acquire at least as many formal qualifications as whites, they do not achieve comparable employment outcomes. Moreover, young Asians and Afro-Caribbeans are more likely to suffer unemployment than their white counterparts (C. Brown 1984).

Finally, with regard to their experience of the labour market, there is less concern in Britain with young people "floundering." As we have seen, during the early and mid-1980s the majority of school leavers experienced spells of unemployment. But this is perceived less as floundering on the part of young people than as an inevitable part of the process of transition at a time when there were just not enough jobs to go around.

Of course, some groups are much more at risk than others; for example, those with few qualifications who enter semi-skilled and unskilled jobs have spells of unemployment more often than those who enter professional, managerial, or technical jobs (Ashton et al. 1990). But the problem is defined by the authorities as one of adjustment; the objective of government programs is not so much to raise young people's aspirations and help them achieve higher-status jobs as to help them adjust their aspirations and expectations to the reality of labour market conditions; hence the location of the YTS within the context of the labour market where young people could learn to adjust to the demands and routines of regular work, while off-the-job training consisted for many of the acquisition of social and life skills. These are defined as the attitudinal and behavioural requirements that employers and others in authority thought necessary for a successful adaptation to work (Lee et al. 1990).

Government Programs

Within this very different British context I shall now turn to various schemes that bear some similarity to the Canadian cooperative programs. Within education these are TVEI and work experience.

Work experience is generally perceived as worthwhile by students and teachers. For young people it provides "a taste of real life" and is seen as relevant. However, it appears to have very little, if any, impact in terms of labour market outcomes. For example, it does not improve the chances of entering higher-status jobs or avoiding unemployment (Hoskins et al. 1989). The one proviso here is that the measures used in the evaluation are not as sophisticated as those adopted in the Canadian study.

Similarly, participation in the Technical Vocational Education Initiative offers young working-class pupils a more relevant curriculum and makes school a more pleasurable and bearable experience. However, it does not necessarily improve the students' performance in public examinations or increase their participation in education past the age of 16 (Bell and Howieson 1988).

Significantly, the scheme that is expected to improve both school performance by the more disadvantaged and their success in the labour market is the COMPACT program, which is currently being introduced. Under this program employers provide a guarantee of specific jobs to young people in return for their achieving a specified level of academic performance. The main concentration of resources aimed at helping the disadvantaged young person in Britain has been through the YTS. Within the scheme, those with such disadvantages as a poor school record are provided with special places for which the government pays the employer a premium.

The effectiveness of this provision has been difficult to evaluate because the allocation of "premium places" has been influenced by the difficulties experienced at a local level in placing young people. Yet these difficulties have less to do with the personal disadvantages of the young person than with local levels of unemployment. Areas of high unemployment tend to be given a high proportion of premium places to entice employers to make provision. But there is no evidence that such areas have a higher proportion of disadvantaged young people.

Conclusion

One of the main conclusions to emerge from this brief survey of the transition from school to work in Britain is that, despite some superficial similarities, none of the programs in the UK are similar to the Canadian co-op program. The main component of that program – the integration of work experience into an educational program for which academic credentials are awarded – has been split and handled differently. Work experience has been introduced into schools, but primarily as a "stand alone" exercise. There has been no attempt to integrate it into an academic or vocational program that is recognized by public forms of certification. Vocational education has been introduced through TVEI but that has no work experience component. New forms of certification that are being introduced involve a large work experience component, but this is being done through YTS, where the emphasis is on young people learning specific work-related skills and the relevant behavioural and attitudinal attributes.

The idea of creating a student-centred program aimed at integrating education and productive work is not necessarily alien in the British context, but given the forms and philosophy of government intervention, it is difficult to implement. The aims of intervention in Britain are not so much to help the student find his or her way through the system as to assist the "trainee" to adjust to the realities of the labour market. This is a fundamentally different approach to the way the problem is defined, one that is rooted in differences in the ideology and class structures of the two societies.

The British model offers one route for overcoming the distinction between traditional education, which emphasizes academic disciplines, and a pragmatic approach that stresses preparation for work. Once out of school, large numbers of youth are served by this means. A very different model exists in Sweden, based on its equalitarian values.

TRANSITION TO WORK IN SWEDEN[2]
RUNE AXELSSON AND ERIK WALLIN

One central characteristic of the transition to work among Swedish youth is the close relationship between work and the schools. We will give a short description of how that relationship is achieved, along with examples of measures taken within and outside the school.

"Short school" means the nine-year comprehensive school for students between the ages of seven and 16, while the gymnasium, or upper secondary school, provides for older students from 16 to

18. The latter encompasses courses of preparation for further theoretical studies but also courses for vocational training. Almost 90 percent of a cohort go on to secondary education, a majority to vocational training/education. Curricula (syllabuses) are centrally determined and followed all over the country, although decentralization is presently taking place.

In the reforms that have taken place since 1950, the relationship between school and working life has been an important issue both as praxis and as ideology. The relationship begins with the lower grades of the comprehensive school. The present curriculum states that schools should be integrated with working life. This means study visits and excursions to places of work and the inclusion of work-related materials in the classroom. Teachers are encouraged to invite representatives from industry and other spheres to take part in teaching. Elderly people are also asked to share their experiences with the pupils.

In grades seven to nine youngsters begin their "practical orientation to working life." Each pupil spends a minimum of six weeks and a maximum of ten weeks in practical work over three years. They must sample at least three different work sectors, such as the metal trades, paper and forest industry, and office management. Obligatory practical experience has two main purposes. One is to enable pupils to learn about working life so that they are better prepared to choose vocational careers, without being too confined by traditions of gender, status, social heritage, and so on. The other is to help students recognize working life as part of society. Practical experience also addresses the need to prepare students for transition to work through forms of polytechnic education.

The same principles are further developed and elaborated in upper secondary education, especially through vocational education courses. In 1971 an integrated system of upper secondary education replaced the old structure, which consisted of a two-year upper secondary continuation school, a more academically oriented upper secondary school (gymnasium), and voluntary vocational school. This old division grew out of and perpetuated segregation in position and values. Now, concern for equal access has become vital. Further, an integrated upper secondary system offers greater potential to make better use of personnel and material resources.

In the new upper secondary framework, vocational education has been given new content and organization. All regular courses were then to be of two years' duration, while special courses of varying length were introduced. Theoretical courses then were not affected. Recently, most programs have been extended to three years and practical and theoretical sectors have been integrated.

Vocational education in upper secondary schools is built around the "block principle." Vocations of a similar kind are grouped together. The basic block consists of elements that are common to the sphere as a whole. Education is subsequently specialized according to occupation.

One important change is the strong increase in general subjects in vocational education. Swedish, introduction to working life, and physical education are compulsory subjects. Beyond these three, students must choose at least one of several optional subjects of a general character.

"Introduction to Working Life" gives students general background on conditions in the labour market and working life. Students also learn something about social and economic questions, trade unions and other organizations in the employment sector, industrial safety, industrial democracy, staff welfare, and questions relating to cooperation. Certain segments of vocational education are provided in places of work outside schools.

Since 1975 surveys have been carried out by the University of Uppsala to determine how former students viewed their experience (Axelsson 1978, 1979, 1989; Wallin and Axelsson 1982). The surveys took place between one and a half and five years after the students left upper secondary school.

According to the participants' reports, education in the workplace forms part of all vocational courses, but to varying degrees. Only when it exceeded eight weeks were a majority of former students satisfied; most of the others wished that they had had more time in the workplace. They were very positive about the benefits, especially those who at the time of the follow-up were working within the competence area of the courses they had taken. The majority of former students who had not received this type of education wished that they had. Unfortunately, 30 percent of those who had received education in the workplace were not contacted by teachers from school during their placement (Axelsson 1978, 1979, 1989).

Though attitudes were generally very favourable, the young people we interviewed voiced some criticism. Contact between school and workplace was sometimes poor; there were deficiencies in the monitoring of attendance and of the quality of the work they were given to do. Some pointed out that the experience they gained was turned to poor account by their schools; the exigencies of the workplace meant that students could not always obtain information they needed; school teaching and the planned experience of working life were badly synchronized; students were sometimes used as cheap labour.

Students are nonetheless very keen on workplace education, for several reasons. They gain indispensable contact with the world outside school; they have been prepared for the step out into the job market, which is therefore easier to take when the time comes. Education as such has a low profile. Working life is an immense teaching aid, an educational resource with rich potential for all school subjects. The contact between school and work becomes a stimulus for both, a challenge to renewal. Working methods, equipment, social relations in the workplace, the working environment (physical as well as psychological), worker safety – these are made tangible. While still at school, young people in the workplace may observe, question, and shape their own values. Schools can encourage this to happen and follow it up in discussions and debates.

The school's role in workplace education – to prepare and to follow up – is vital. Without this participation workplace education strays from its objectives. The main responsibility ought to rest with the schools; it is a matter of education. It is important for young people to be exposed to a wide variety of work that makes sense from the viewpoint of their education.

The curriculum advocates reciprocal contacts between school and society: "School constitutes a part of society. Through reciprocal contacts between school and the local community, both identify with each other" (Lgy 70 1970, 11, our translation).

The criticism that schools did not make the best use of students' work experiences in their teaching is supported by other data, notably reports by upper secondary school inspectors (Fredriksson 1981, 122).

Referring to our results, Beatrice Reubens (1982) outlines
from a US viewpoint some of what she sees as the most important
trends in foreign countries. "The idea that all young people require initial formal occupational skill training, either in school
or in firms" is meeting with increased acceptance. "There is a
growing unanimity on the need for a large part of the school-
based training to occur in actual workplaces." Meanwhile, "active participation of employer and worker organizations in planning and operating vocational education courses is gaining in
importance." Occupational skill training "begins at a later age
than it previously did," while "career education, general preparation for work, and the transition from school to work have become important in the education of the younger age groups"
(ibid., 69).

Vocational courses provide examples of strong preparation for
transition. The theoretical ones still leave much to be desired.

Out-of-School Initiatives

As stated initially, the main responsibility for easing the transition
to work among young people falls upon the school, but various
measures are taken outside school. These initiatives, generated
and supported by the National Labour Market Board, are directed mainly at young people who for one reason or another are
unemployed, or who want to change careers.

The best known of the programs is the Youth Team. Under the
Youth Teams Act, which came into force in January 1984, those
young people to whom the Employment Service can offer
neither employment, nor education, nor training are entitled to
four hours' paid work per day, usually provided by municipal
authorities, as an alternative to unemployment entitlement.
Young people are eligible for Youth Team work until the age of
20. Program participants must spend two hours a week looking
for jobs.

Entrepreneurial activities may be pursued by youth who wish to
do so. Those over 18 may work in their own businesses for at least
four hours a day instead of being employed in Youth Teams. They
are entitled to a certain weekly payment for their own enterprises
for up to a year. But according to the National Labour Market
Board, very few young people choose the entrepreneurial route.

Moreover, the board points out that, while in theory it is open to young people themselves to create their own Youth Team jobs – for example, by asking a municipal authority whether they could undertake a specific type of job – only rarely does this happen.

The Labour Market Board does fund some out-of-school initiatives that are designed to promote the understanding and practice of enterprise. Two are now described. Since 1983, for example, "the Blade" has offered cooperative-oriented education and training to young unemployed people over 20 through courses that last 63 weeks. The aim is to prepare participants to establish their own worker co-op in the hope, as one of the program's publicity leaflets puts it, that "their sense of guilt and failure at not getting a job" will change into "a belief in their own ability to take care of their own lives." This is achieved through a mix of theory and practice. The theoretical courses include social studies and political education, learning about different forms of business association and organization including co-operatives, Swedish, history (especially the history of ideas, work, and popular movements such as the labour and co-op movements), business administration, finance, and bookkeeping. The practical activities are undertaken in three stages. Throughout, the young people work in the co-op itself, but during the first ten-week stage work takes the form of on-the-job training. During the next ten weeks and thereafter, youth are engaged in productive work activities within the cooperative. During the final 43 weeks the young people, working in groups, begin to identify and plan their own cooperatives. In this way young people can acquire faith in themselves and build self-confidence.

The Varmland Cooperatives foundation, like the Blade, aims at encouraging young people to create jobs through cooperative activity. The courses it offers are also similar and geared towards improving self-confidence, knowledge, and will; imparting a concrete understanding of cooperation, developing enterprise through group relations and vocational skills, and building strong individuals and groups.

A Look Ahead

In 1986 the government's Group for a Review of Upper Secondary Vocational Education suggested that vocational courses should be extended for a third year (SOU 1986). This has recently been done. It was also recommended that students be given a "perspective on life" through insight into "how our society is built up and a knowledge of the democratic rules of the game," the "conditions of working life," and also "central elements of social and family knowledge." This necessitates "a relatively sizeable element of general subjects within the frame of vocational education" (ibid., 153).

Teachers and school management ought to show young people trust and give them responsibility. This may be accomplished by giving students an active part in the planning and implementation of their education. Schools ought to encourage involvement in student unions and train them to exercise their rights and duties regarding working environment issues (ibid., 101).

The review group emphasized that an individual's self-confidence is an important prerequisite if that person is to try to make a difference and demand change. This means "having a feeling that it is possible to learn things that contribute to changing your own situation" (ibid., 100). "Sound self-confidence is essential if students are to experience pleasure in and sense the purpose of their studies" (ibid., 101).

The content, structure, and conduct of vocational education have an important influence on how the organization of work will be developed in the future. "Vocational education should not only prepare students for an occupation but also give them an orientation regarding work in adjacent fields and provide vocational theory and general knowledge which can serve as a basis for further study" (ibid., 100).

Education ought to function as an "instrument of change in working life." It should not be narrowly geared to existing vocational functions. "On the contrary, it must have such breadth that it provides a preparedness to meet changes in working life and can function as a basis for continuing education" (ibid., 130).

Vocational education that is entirely school- or work-centred has major drawbacks. "A combination is therefore preferred, utilizing the advantages of each system" (ibid., 110). All vocational education ought to contain some element of workplace education – the review group suggested at least ten percent would be an appropriate average. For some courses a higher percentage is justifiable. Transferring certain vocational elements from school to workplace could, according to the group, give vocational teachers time for their own compulsory in-service education, and for keeping in touch with students gaining experience off campus (ibid., 113).

Students must be given a realistic view of what is expected in working life. School and workplace education must be made more complementary. This could be accomplished through regular collaboration between teachers and employees of the firms concerned. Teachers must be given the opportunity to study work education results in their particular area, as well as in education generally. This would minimize the risk of excessively conservative or excessively utopian assessments of working life by all concerned (ibid., 103).

Teachers must be trained to "help students critically reflect upon and work through their experiences, establish background and proportion to their experiences, and relate them to the knowledge which they encounter in the classroom and in learning aids." Skill training or social and cultural notions in workplaces can constitute important links in the development of knowledge and personality (ibid., 200).

The group's basic view is that school and work have a common responsibility for vocational education, while the overriding responsibility rests with the state. There should be close cooperation between personnel in schools and other workplaces. Teachers of related subjects should plan this cooperation, monitor developments, and maintain continual contact with instructors in the workplace. The teacher at school and the instructor in the workplace should have opportunities for work exchanges.

Snapshots from Follow-Up Studies

Follow-up studies constitute a broad overall evaluation of all courses of study. Regardless of how long they have been out of school, respondents show a very stable pattern. Students who took vocational courses in upper secondary school indicate that the courses were "good, but could have been better." (Criticism by young people of shortcomings in workplace education in terms of synchronization, meaningfulness, and follow-up is echoed in other countries.) Among the former students who were surveyed, 90 percent reported satisfaction with the vocational education they received, and 60 percent reported satisfaction with the associated general education they received.

The self-confidence of those who had taken theoretical courses did not increase. In fact the opposite is the case. In part this may be because students tend to blame themselves when they find it difficult to understand something.

Former vocational students also expressed security in their abilities, especially in their vocational areas. There are two reasons for this. First, students were given tasks that were difficult enough to stimulate but easy enough to manage, and that had a clear end. The more significant reason is that the pupils in vocational education had been given enough time to learn their lessons and do their tasks thoroughly enough to be able to say: "I know this! I know how to do this." This forms a base for skill security and self-confidence.

Again, respondents who had taken the three-year theoretical courses felt less secure. It is not that they were dissatisfied with their degree of preparation for further studies or for their present jobs; rather, they wished for more contact with the surrounding society. This is a dissatisfaction with methods. Many former theoretical-line students said that they had not been encouraged to draw their own conclusions, to discuss, to take responsibility for learning, to try to get broad overviews of different fields, or to foster a questioning attitude. They talk of "stamping in the sausage." They acquired knowledge but did not experience it as their own, as part of themselves, to help them live their lives.

The findings indicate that young people who are involved in educational activities that include some form of practice involving learner responsibility, and that are "difficult enough to stimulate, easy enough to manage," as Wallin aptly put it (1982), feel that such features improve their self-confidence and sense of security in what they know.

There is surely reason for apprehension about new technologies sweeping away the traces of the craft foundation on which, historically, the Swedish economy rests. Workplace education is borne up by the pragmatic perspective – knowledge is applied to problems in the school's immediate vicinity, the community, and the economy. Some argue that the knowledge-centred perspective hardly leaves room for workplace education; cognitive knowledge is considered to be of supreme value, and its practical application is beyond the remit of schools. Yet workplace education may offer opportunities for constructive criticism of society and of the relations prevailing in society and in working life.

It may be the case that polytechnical education under communist hegemony in East European states excluded economic and political conditions that, in practical terms, are conflict-laden. In broad terms, polytechnical education should have three elements: a cognitive element, through which students learn that science and technology are important to economic growth and make acquaintance with important sectors of industry; a moral element, whereby students are taught to respect the value of work; and a practical element, in which students learn basic skills.

Implicit or "tacit" knowledge is not completely conscious; many hold that it cannot be achieved effectively in an artificial classroom setting. Workplace education may serve an important function in this respect.

Students who participated in our evaluations gave priority to the "skills knowledge" they had gained through workplace education. School activities centre around "statement knowledge" – the theoretical, sometimes unnecessarily abstract, description of an activity or phenomenon. Statement knowledge may dominate at school but students feel the need to supplement it with skills knowledge. In terms of decision making and practice, it is fair to say that theoretical courses have a lot to learn from vocational education and training. It is partly through the acquisition of skills knowledge and learning from example and tradition that students get the chance to develop the competence that is so important for self-confidence. Students want more of this kind of learning and more skills knowledge. Workplace education has the potential to give it to them. It will also ease the transition from school to work. However, in order to counteract indoctrination and restrictive specialization, it is important for schools to exercise supervision over and have responsibility for education located in industry.

CHAPTER TEN

Findings and Conclusions

What is learned in school depends far less on what is
taught than on what is experienced.
Edgar Friedenberg

One distinctive feature of *On Their Own?* is that it analyzes interaction between structures of transition to work and the values and experiences of individual youth. The enquiry began with four questions:

1 What opportunities are provided youth to prepare for employment that is steady, rewarding, and fulfilling?
2 How do youth respond to these opportunities or lack of them?
3 How do class, gender, and ethnicity affect transition?
4 What policies and programs widen opportunities and motivate young people to take advantage of them?

This final chapter reviews major findings related to these questions and proposes measures to smooth the launch into productive and gratifying adulthood.

Our analysis has two basic elements. It defines and describes the actual dimensions of transition and then looks at the main conditions for a positive transition. These conditions include background or structural factors such as social status, gender, ethnicity, and the influence of others as expressed in their hopes for young people's attainment. They also include personal variables like youth's job hopes, marks, basic beliefs, and effort.

DIMENSIONS OF TRANSITION

Outcomes or dimensions that are important for transition include educational attainment, present job level, job goal, innovative career planning, stable employment, intrinsic satisfaction and on-the-job training.

Educational attainment It has been noted that our young adult sample is purposive and not fully representative of the general population. We might expect them to surpass the average in attainment and they do. Almost 30 percent had reached or graduated from university, 20 percent had been to college, and 30 percent had just a high school diploma. Under 20 percent left without one, compared with 30 percent across the country a few years earlier. This did not include the 11 percent who were still studying. Most new jobs use computers and require post-secondary education.

Present job level Many jobs held by youth are temporary or part time and pay little. Better jobs are won partly as a result of planning realistically for ten years hence and attaining the necessary higher education and marks, blending structures and individual factors. Other significant antecedents to good jobs are a close fit between schooling and job and maternal occupation. Girls and minorities are at a job disadvantage in spite of having slightly more education than boys and similarly high hopes.

Five years after high school, 35 percent of young adults in our sample were in semi-skilled or unskilled jobs and 31 percent in skilled posts; 18 percent were supervisors, managers, professionals, or owners, while 17 percent were not in the workforce. At this stage educational level is not yet a powerful predictor of job level, partly because many are still studying and partly because it takes years to establish a permanent position. But education is still the strongest predictor of job rank.

Job hopes While in high school, most youth had job goals that turned out to be unrealistically high. Very few aimed at skilled jobs. Instead, the largest group hoped to become professionals or executives of medium or large-sized firms. While most had not yet reached these heights – few ever do – strong, high hopes motivated effort and helped them win good marks and plan to take further training.

Innovative career planning   Challenging work that requires retraining from time to time was the preference for 38 percent of our young adults, indicating their readiness for employment in the information age. Antecedents significantly associated with this position include father's help, minority origin, and closeness of fit between education and job.

Stable employment   This and its opposite – *unemployment* – reflect the fluidity of the youth labour market. Young entrants in North America typically flounder for a few years, caught in discontinuities between market demand and their qualifications and goals. Lacking experience, they are extremely vulnerable. Surprisingly, the best predictor of stable employment is democratic decision making in the family. Youth accustomed to consultative planning at home are more resilient than others in seeking and holding jobs. Stable employment is also the result of higher education, paternal help and consonance in elders' aspirations for youth. However, one-half of the youth sample had been unemployed, on average for over three months.

Intrinsic satisfaction   Interest in meaningful, challenging work is associated significantly with maternal education, a young person's marks, educational level, and flexible gender norms – a blend of structural and individual normative variables.

On-the-job training   The fact that less than one-quarter of employers offer a month or more of on-the-job training – a proportion replicated across the country – prevents construction of a rational, reliable model to explain this dimension of transition. The only significant predictor is gender; women receive less training than men. Public services and firms that use high tech are most apt to offer on-the-job training. Smaller firms sometimes subsidize off-site courses.

Part-Time Work during Term

Over 80 percent of the youth sample worked during term – on average 19 hours a week. One reason was to support a consumerist lifestyle, although many drew satisfaction from this other role as an indication of their growing maturity and independence. But they had little time for leisure. Working over 16 hours a week was significantly related with dropping out, low marks, and the attainment of less education. Parents seem unaware of these hazards and feel that part-time jobs after school keep kids out of trouble and teach them responsibility. Teachers see the dangers. Forty percent of youth who had worked long hours admit that their studies had suffered.

THE ROOT QUESTIONS

Returning to the four basic questions addressed here, the first, about opportunities, must be answered conditionally. Youth typically said, "There are jobs out there but they are hard to find and keep." Only slightly more than half of parents were considered by their children to have been helpful in transition. Peers were next, followed by teachers and, lastly, employers.

Only about half of the youth said that they worked hard or moderately hard at school, though, paradoxically, four-fifths said they themselves were chiefly responsible for their transition. Three-quarters said they were committed to careers.

As for the effects of underlying social structures, this study confirms what others have found. Social class has a persistent though indirect impact on outcomes. Girls work harder at school, get better grades, and go further but are often handicapped in the job market. The same holds for visible minorities.

Finally, what can be done to improve transition? There is broad consensus that co-operative education should be taken by all or most students; its usefulness has been clearly demonstrated. A minority of secondary school teachers, usually not familiar with co-op, oppose reforms that would align education more closely with community and business. A minority of employers think that they would benefit from closer relations with schools, though many, especially in small firms, had not even heard of co-op.

CONDITIONS FOR ATTAINMENT

Background and others' influence   The impact of social class, gender, and ethnicity on transition, firmly supported in other research, is clearly demonstrated here. Youth from high-status families have an advantage in extended education and job-entry level. Girls and certain minorities such as Orientals and East Asians excel in education but do not do as well as white, Anglo-Saxon men in early occupations. However, the impact of these structural conditions is indirect. They work through individual characteristics such as marks, occupational goals, effort, and values such as worship, efficacy of norms at school and work, and preference for equity in sex roles.

Fifty percent of parents, often unrealistically, told their children they hoped they would go to university. Seventeen percent mentioned college and 33 percent would be content if their children obtained a high school diploma. Teachers were not so optimistic. Thirty percent, according to young adults, urged university as a goal, ten percent suggested college, and 20 percent a high school diploma, while 40 percent did not say.

Sixty-three percent of mothers were said to be very helpful, fathers came next at 53 percent, followed by spouses or peers, then teachers. Employers were not often considered to have been helpful in transition.

Job hopes and reality   Many youth and parents, again often unrealistically, especially among those not involved in co-op education, aspired to high positions. Nearly half of our youth believed that ten years down the road they would be managers, professionals, or owners. Thirty percent of parents shared their dreams. Teachers were closer to reality but few talked with students about skilled jobs. Employers who were not involved in co-op tended to be pessimistic or silent about our sample's future ranks.

Forty percent of parents and two-thirds of teachers never talked with students about careers; some parents didn't feel qualified and others didn't want to impose leads on the next generation. Many teachers didn't think it was their responsibility. But young people often took silence to mean indifference or scepticism.

Marks and basic values   The strongest direct antecedent of educational and work attainment was not structural but individual –

marks! This was followed by feasible job goals, then background, help from others, and the youth's own values and beliefs. About 60 percent said they practised their beliefs at work. Ethical practice correlates with higher marks, as does attendance at worship. Both value orientations also contribute towards anticipated intrinsic satisfaction with work.

Those with active values and beliefs seem to be inner driven in performance; this leads to productive and fulfilling careers. In our sample, students of this type began to take charge of their future by the age of about 17, usually by Grade Eleven.

Consonance in others' expectations For about half of our young adults, there was consonance or consistency in the educational and job goals held for them by parents and teachers. Again, remember this is a purposive sample, overrepresenting subjects with access to schools in middle- and working-class areas that had cooperative education programs. Consonance between parents and employers fell to about one-third. It was higher – one-half – between teachers and employers but fell to about one-quarter between all three socializing agents. Goal consonance was stronger among those from higher-status families. It leads to greater effort, higher marks, and attainment at school and early jobs.

Cooperative education Though they tend to come from lower-status families, co-op students attained marks almost as high as other students. More and more university-bound students enrol in co-op, usually for career exploration. Such students made up 40 percent of enrolments in 1989–90 at the time of our interviews. They gave parents and teachers more credit for help in transition than others did from similar backgrounds. Co-op raised attainment in education and jobs, increased self-confidence, and helped graduates find work that was more consistent with their schooling.

CONCLUSION

Observations by participants in the study and reflection on effective measures in the United Kingdom and Sweden lead to proposals for structural changes in education and training, most of which substantiate those urged in earlier studies. Our contribution, after extensive field observation, is to specify the need and readiness for change and the directions it should take. The subjects – youth, parents, former teachers, and many employers – provide grounds for these recommendations, which were expressed several years before the OECD published similar proposals. Here is evidence to support proposals for reform by Ontario, Alberta, British Columbia, and other ministries of Education.

Streaming at Grade Nine is premature and hinders many young, inexperienced Canadians who seek a way into occupations that fit their aspirations and qualifications. A common core curriculum for all students from Grades Nine to Eleven should replace present tiered systems. From Grade Twelve on there should be a choice of specialized programs suited to students' abilities and goals, in the light of market opportunities.

By the time students reach secondary school, most have formed attitudes towards education and their own futures that are random at best and often unrealistic or negative. To acquaint them with possible careers and to help them discover their inner resources, all middle school students should take short work-and-community courses. Through Grades Seven, Eight, and Nine there should be a required program of 8 to 10 weeks on community and careers, with a major component of work education. This might include job observation, shadowing, and mentoring at several work sites in various sectors.

Work education curricula should refer to the social situation and environment of students, yet relate personal and local knowledge to wider understanding. The human and material resources that every community has should be enlisted to enrich what is done in schools to enhance transition.

Many schools have councils and advisory groups that include older students or recent graduates, parents, employers, and representatives of occupational and voluntary groups. These should be given a meaningful part in the planning, supporting, and monitoring of transitional programs.

Cooperative education should be a required course in upper secondary school. Its benefits have been demonstrated in this and other research. Most students, educators, parents, and employers in the study favour the expansion of the co-op program to include all or most students.

One serious obstacle for some is the time devoted by students to paid part-time work during term, usually unrelated to studies. In northern Europe learning allowances are paid to students in skilled programs; they should be introduced here. This is advocated by the OECD (1996A) and ministries of Education in several provinces. It would strengthen mutual commitment between student, educator, and employer, raise the effectiveness of learning, and help generate well-qualified workers, technicians, managers, and professionals.

Tax incentives, which are in place in Sweden, the UK, France, and elsewhere, would make advanced training programs equitable and attractive here. It has been shown that the cost benefit of such schemes is higher when most of the training is practised at work sites, with theoretical instruction in schools or institutes (OECD 1996A).

In the view of most of our interviewees, restructuring is essential to prepare students, including returnees, for productive, fulfilling careers in the information age. As education faces cuts by governments overburdened by debt charges, change is inevitable. While schools must control transitional curricula, collaboration with employers and communities is the way to go.

Notes

CHAPTER ONE

1 Scales for consonance in goals, or aspirations for students' education
and jobs that were held by parents, teachers, and employers, were
constructed by assigning scores of 1 for low, 2 for medium, and 3 for
high levels for each case and adding them to arrive at a total score.
Then a scale of overall consonance was computed for each case by
adding the separate consonance scores of influential others for aspirations on education and job. The overall consonance score was more
strongly related with positive transitional dimensions than were separate consonance scores held by different others.

CHAPTER THREE

1 Social resistance refers to the ways individuals acquire practical
knowledge of the social order through their labour and communi-
cative action in order to manipulate these structures to their own
ends.
2 The concept of contradiction has been defined by Giddens (1979)
as "principles which operate in terms of everyone but at the same
time contravene one another." Contradictions have a dual location:
(a) they exist in the principles of institutional life that make social
action possible; (b) they exist in the principles, practices, and experiences constituted by social action.
3 King and Hughes 1985; William T. Grant Foundation 1988; United
States General Accounting Office 1990.

CHAPTER FOUR

1 As a percentage of gross national product, Canada's expenditure on public education in 1992, 7.6 percent, exceeded that of the United States (5.3 in 1989), France (5.7 in 1992), the United Kingdom (5.2 in 1991), and Japan (4.7 in 1989). It is less than in Sweden (8.8 in 1992) and Norway (8.7 in 1992). It is slightly higher than in Denmark – 7.4 in 1991 (UNESCO, 1994, Statistical Yearbook, Section 2.10). The greater role of private education in the United States, France, the United Kingdom, and Japan helps to explain differences with Canada. In Japan competition for advancement is stronger than in other advanced countries and many large firms have their own schools and colleges.

CHAPTER FIVE

1 Anisef et al. 1982, chapter 2, "Accessibility: the Public Debate."
2 The practice of experiential learning is widespread in Canadian secondary schools, specifically through the spread of work education and cooperative learning. It is growing comparatively slowly in universities and its progress in colleges of applied arts and technology is uncharted, except in Quebec. There it has become approved practice in the CEGEP system, the credits being transferable to universities. Canada is years behind the UK, the United States, and Nordic countries in opening universities to unconventional learning for credit. References include Alan Thomas 1989; Kolb 1984; Slavin 1990; and Simon et al. 1991.
3 Many studies in Canada and elsewhere show that there is a consistent relationship between length and level of education and social class. Some of these studies were mentioned in chapter 3.
4 Anisef et al. 1982.

CHAPTER SIX

1 Canadian business spent 0.8 percent of gross domestic product on Research and Development in 1991, far behind Japan at 2.2 percent, the United States (1.9 percent), Germany (1.8 percent), and Sweden at 1.6 percent (Squires 1995).
2 Crysdale et al. 1998. Full-time work in Canada increased in 1994 by about 430,000 jobs, "but not one of them went to youth under 25. The older group got there first" (Bruce Little 1995B).

CHAPTER EIGHT

1 It is impossible to compare the distribution of education in the sample with census tract data because of the special nature of the sample. It consists of young people between the ages of 22 and 25, in four highly urbanized industrial areas, almost half of whom have been in co-op education. Further, the sample is drawn from ten schools that are in middle-working-class basins. Then, as mentioned in chapter 1, it underrepresents dropouts and very mobile youth. But so do census figures.

CHAPTER NINE

1 This section was written by David N. Ashton of the Centre for Labour Market Studies, University of Leicester, UK.
2 This section was written by Rune Axelsson and Erik Wallin of the Faculty of Education at Uppsala University in Sweden.

APPENDIX

Table A–1
Occupational Aspirations for Individuals in Sample and Present Job (Percentages)

	Rated by				
	Parents	Teachers	Employers	Self	Present Job
Unskilled, semi-skilled	3	6	11	2	35
Skilled blue/white collar	17	5	17	25	31
Manager, small firm, supervisor, medium-size firm	3	3	3	18	11
Manager, medium-size firm, professional	29	19	8	49	7
No plans, don't know, other	48	67	61	7	17*
Totals	100	100	100	101	101
Frequencies	(324)	(324)	(324)	(324)	(324)

* Six percent of the youth sample were looking for work and 11 percent were students.

Table A–2
Marks, Effort at School, Background, and Co-op Education Score (r-Correlations)

	Marks	Effort at School
Mother's education	–	–
Father's education	.120*	–
Mother's occupation	.161*	–
Father's occupation	–	–
Parents' ethnicity (minority)	.170**	–
Gender	.119*	.096*
Mothers' help	.164**	.353***
Fathers' help	.133*	.167*
Teachers' help	–	.130*
Self-help	.189**	–
Effort at school	.374***	1.000
Positive co-op education score	–	.193

*   Significant at the .05 level.
**   Significant at the .001 level.
***   Significant at the .0001 level.

Table A–3
Youth's Values and Transitional Outcomes; Belief Efficacy and Religious Practice
(r-Correlations)

	Efficacy/Beliefs at Work	Attendance Religious Services
1 Marks, last secondary year	.216*	.199*
2 Job expectation	–	–
3 Pay, weekly, full time	.129*	–
4 Intrinsic satisfaction, expected job	.143**	.124*
5 Efficacy, beliefs at work	1.000	.111*

*   Significant at the .05 level.
**   Significant at the .001 level.

Table A–4
Influence of Father, Mother, and Both on Youth's Early Attainments (r-Correlations)

Youth's Attainments	Father			Mother			Aspirations of Both	
	Education	Occupation	Help	Education	Occupation	Help	Education	Occupation
Effort at school			.144*					
Self-help in transition					.137*	.357***	.123*	.210*
Job aspiration	.249***	.228***		.252***	.253***	.137*	.387***	.480***
Marks, secondary school	.117*		.123*		.171*	.175*	.204**	.354***
Education level	.308***	.223*	.169**	.256***	.308***		.350***	.468***
Present job level	.137*	.207**		.261***	.330***		.273**	.273**

* = r significant at the .05 level, **at the .001 level, ***at the .0001 level.

The strongest correlations for comparable items are usually between youth's attainments and aspirations jointly held by both parents, as shown in the right-hand columns.

Table A–5
Occupational Aspiration in Ten Years and Present Job, Correlated with
Background and Present Job (r-Correlations)

	Occupational Aspiration	*Present Job*
Mother's education	.216***	.211***
Father's education	.208***	.130*
Mother's occupation	.304***	.323***
Father's occupation	.241***	.214***
Gender†	–	–.104*
Mothers' help	.118*	–
Father's help	.126*	–
Teacher's help	–	–
Present Job	.414***	1.000

* Significant at the .05 level.
** Significant at the .001 level.
*** Significant at the .0001 level.
† Minus sign indicates feminine gender.

Table A–6
Final Secondary Marks and Educational Attainment, by Gender (Percentages)

Marks		*Boys*	*Girls*
Under 60		8	3
60–9		37	29
70–9		37	51
80–93		17	17
Total	%	99	100
Frequencies		(145)	(174)
$X_2 = 9.89$, df 3, p <.0195			
Mean marks		68.9	71.8
Significant at the <.024 level.			
Educational Attainment			
No diploma		21	9
Grade Twelve, Thirteen		28	32
Post-secondary, some or complete college		19	24
University, some or graduation		32	35
Total	%	100	100
Frequencies		(145)	
$X_2 = 9.05$, df 3, p <.029			

Table A–7
Present Job Level, Monthly Pay and Length of Job Training, by Gender
(Percentages)

		Men	Women
Present job level, means*		41.7	40.3
Difference not significant			
Monthly pay			
Under $400		27	56
$400–499		27	25
$500 and over		46	20
Total	%	100	101
Frequencies		(43)	(126)
X_2 = 23.907, df 2, p <.00001			
Means of monthly pay		$589	$367
Significant at the .057 level			
Length of job training			
None or under one week		53	64
One week to one month		20	20
Over one month		28	16
Total	%	101	100
Frequencies		(131)	(162)
X_2 = 6.103, df 2, p .047			

* Job level is based on the Blishen Occupational Scale, in which scores of 40 are lower than
   average. This reflects the transitional nature of youth's present jobs.

Table A–8
Pay, Job Training, Job Expected, and Anticipated Job Satisfaction by Social Class, Gender, and Ethnicity (r-Correlations)

	Full-time Pay	Length of Job Training	Job Expectation	Anticipated Intrinsic Satisfaction
Mother's education			.216***	.232***
Father's education			.208***	.103*
Mother's occupation	.143*	.143*	.304***	.169**
Father's occupation			.241***	.113*
Gender (female)	−.335***	−.134*		.100*
Ethnicity (minority)			.103*	

* Significant at the .05 level.
** Significant at the .001 level.
*** Significant at the .0001 level.

Table A–9
The Impact of Intermediate Experiences and Background on Youth's Educational Level (r-Correlations)

	Youth's Education*
INTERMEDIATE EXPERIENCES	
Average marks, last high school year	.472
Youth's job aspirations	.410
BACKGROUND	
Parent's aspirations for youth's jobs	.376
Father's education	.306
Mother's occupation	.302
Teacher's educational aspirations	.281
Employer's educational aspirations	.261
Mother's education	.261
Father's occupation	.258

* All correlations here are significant at the .0001 level.

Table A–10
Correlates of Close Fit between School Course and Planned Job (r-Correlations)

Effort at school	.151**
Peer help	.160**
Average marks	.209***
Educational attainment	.191**
Present job level	.243***
Unemployment	−.220***
Intrinsic satisfaction with present job	.211***
Pay	.168**
Job-hunt worries	−.198**
Employers' educational hopes	.264***
Consonance, overall aspirations of elders	.171**
General satisfaction	.243***
Positive co-op rating	.291***
Innovative career plans	.238***

** Significant at the .001 level.
*** Significant at the .0001 level.

Table A–11
Significant Correlations between Transitional Outcomes and Substantial
Job-Hunt Worries (r-Correlations)

Self-help in setting goals and reaching them	−.218***
Average marks, last year at high school	−.159**
Employers' educational aspirations	−.139**
Intrinsic ideal job satisfaction	−.146**
Intrinsic satisfaction with present job	−.154**
Education attainment	−.091*
Length of unemployment	.164**
Pay, last full-time job	−.216***
Innovative career plans	−.163**

Negative correlation means that less of the outcome is correlated with more job hunt worry.
* Significant at the .06 level.
** Significant at the .001 level.
*** Significant at the .0001 level.

Table A–12
Correlates of Prolonged Unemployment (r-Correlations)

ANTECEDENTS	
Mother's occupation	–.143*
Father's help in transition	–.219***
Average marks, last year in high school	–.207***
Teachers' educational aspirations	–.134*
Employers' job aspirations	–.231**
Youth's own job aspirations	–.168**
Educational attainment	–.261***
Intrinsic satisfaction, ideal job	–.157**
Intrinsic satisfaction, last job	–.156**
CONSEQUENCES	
Present job level	–.168**
Job-hunt worries	.164**
Views on technology's effects on jobs	–.164**

Negative correlation means that more of the correlate is associated with less unemployment.
*   Significant at the .01 level.
**   Significant at the .001 level.
*** Significant at the .0001 level.

Table A–13
Regression on Education

Rank, by significance	Independent variable	Beta coefficient	Partial coefficient	Significance T
1	All marks, final year	.3391	.3502	.0000
2	Youth's job hopes	.2047	.2244	.0009
3	Peer help	.1317	.1575	.0202
4	Consonance, all elders' aspirations	.1388	.1547	.0226

R^2 = 3.61, f 215 (cases). Significances of under .05 are conventionally reliable.

Table A–14
Regression on Present Job

Rank, by significance	Independent variable	Beta coefficient	Partial coefficient	Significance T
1	Job expectation	.3011	.3101	.0000
2	Courses closely related to job	.1887	.2101	.0021
3	Mother's occupation	.1713	.1913	.0052
4	Sex (female)*	−.1254	−.1436	.0367

R^2 = .270, f 210.
* Negative regression means females had lower-level jobs.

Table A–15
Regression on Innovativeness in Career Planning

Rank, by significance	Independent variable	Beta coefficient	Partial coefficient	Significance T
1	Present job	.2948	.3019	.0000
2	Father's help	.1842	.1994	.0036
3	Father's ethnicity, non-anglo/franco	.1449	.1592	.0204
4	Courses closely related to job	.1349	.1440	.0362

R^2 = .200, f 210.

Table A–16
Regression on Unemployment

Rank, by significance	Independent variable	Beta coefficient	Partial coefficient	Significance T
1	Democratic decision making in family	−.2153	−.2169	.0009
2	Father's education	.1925	.1928	.0031
3	Youth's education	−.1860	−.1852	.0046
4	Father's help	−.1380	−.1416	.0307
5	Consonance in elder's hopes	−.1265	−.1272	.0526

R^2 = .158, f 231.
Minus sign indicates negative relationship.

Table A–17
Regression on Pay

Rank, by significance	Independent variable	Beta coefficient	Partial coefficient	Significance T
1	Females*	–.3454	–.3681	.0000
2	Present job	.0431	.0474	.0045

R^2 = .256, f 189.

* Negative coefficient means females received lower pay.

Bibliography

Angus Reid Group. 1993. *The Religion Poll. Toronto.* Toronto.

Anisef, Paul, J.G. Paasche, and A.H. Turrittin. 1980. *Is the Die Cast?: Educational Achievements and Work Destinations of Ontario Youth.* Toronto: Ministry of Colleges and Universities.

Anisef, Paul, N. Okihiro, and C. James. 1982. *Losers and Winners: The Pursuit of Equality and Social Justice in Higher Education.* Toronto: Butterworths.

Anisef, Paul. 1990. *The Transition from School to Work: Educational and Occupational Status Attainments of Youth.* Toronto: Ministry of Skills Development.

Anisef, Paul, and Paul Axelrod, eds. 1993. *Transitions: Schooling and Employment in Canada.* Toronto: Thompson Educational Publishing.

Althusser, L. 1969. *For Marx.* Harmondsworth: Penguin.

Anyon, Jean. 1983. "Intersections of Gender and Class: Accommodation and Resistance by Working-Class and Affluent Females in Contradictory Sex-Role Ideologies." In Stephen Walker and Len Barton. *Gender, Class and Education.* London: Falmer Press.

Armstrong, Pat, and Hugh Armstrong. 1994. *Double Ghetto: Canadian Women at Their Segregated Work.* Toronto: McClelland and Stewart.

Ashton, D.N., and D. Field. 1976. *Young Workers: The Transition from School to Work.* London: Hutchinson.

Ashton, D.N., and M.J. Maguire. 1988. *Young Adults in the Labour Market.* Research Paper 55. London: Department of Employment.

Ashton, D.N., F. Green, and M. Hoskins. 1988. "The Training System of British Capitalism: Changes and Prospects." In *The Restructuring of the*

UK Economy, edited by F. Green. Hemel Hempstead: Harvester Wheat-sheaf.

Ashton, D.N., M.J. Maguire, and M. Spilsbury. 1990. *Restructuring the Labour Market: The Implications for Youth*. London: Macmillan.

Ashton, David, and Graham Lowe. eds. 1991. *Making Their Way: Education, Training and the Labour Market in Canada and Britain*. Toronto and Buckingham: University of Toronto Press/Open University Press.

Axelrod, Paul, and Paul Anisef. 1991. *The Transition from School to Work: A Bibliography*. Toronto: York University.

− 1995. *Transitions, the Life Course and the Class of '75: Implications for Social Policy*. Toronto: York University.

Axelsson, R. 1978. "Vocational Education in the Swedish Upper Secondary School: An Evaluation." *Pedagogist Forskning Uppsala* 1. Uppsala: Department of Education, Uppsala University.

− 1979. "Evaluation of Vocational Education in the Swedish Upper Secondary School." *Scandinavian Journal of Educational Research* 23, no. 4: 169–84.

− 1989. "Upper Secondary School in Retrospect: The View of Former Students." *Acta Univeritatus Upsaliensis, Uppsala Studies in Education* 30, Uppsala: Department of Education, Uppsala University.

Bachman, J.G., L.D. Johnston, and R.M. O'Malley. 1987. *Monitoring the Future*. Ann Arbor: Survey Research Institute, University of Michigan.

Baichman-Anisef, E., Paul Anisef, and P. Axelrod. 1993. *The Transition from School to Work: A Bibliography*. Toronto: York University Institute for Social Research.

Bandura, Albert. 1971. *Social Learning Theory*. Englewood Cliffs, NJ: Prentice-Hall.

Banting, K.G., and C.M. Beach, eds. 1995. *Labour Market Polarization and Social Policy Reform*. Kingston, ON: School of Policy Studies, Queen's University.

Beiser, Morton, Phyllis Johnson, and Daniel Roshi. 1994. *The Mental Health of Southeast Asian Refugees in Canada*. Toronto: Clarke Institute of Psychiatry.

Bell, C., and C. Howieson. 1988. "The View from the Hutch." In *Education and the Youth Labour Market*, edited by D. Raffe. Lewes: Falmer.

Bernstein, Basil. 1977. *Class, Codes and Control*. London: Routledge and Kegan Paul.

Betcherman, Gordon, Kathryn McMullen, Norm Leckie, and Christina Caron. 1994A. *The Canadian Workplace in Transition*. Kingston, ON: Industrial Relations Centre, Queen's University.

Betcherman, Gordon, and René Morissette. 1994B. *Recent Youth Labour Market Experiences.* Ottawa: Business and Labour Market Analysis Group, Statistics Canada.

Bibby, Reginald W., and Donald Posterski. 1985. *The Emerging Generation.* Toronto: Irwin.

– 1992. *Teen Trends.* Toronto: Stoddart.

Bloom, Michael. 1995. *Ethical Questions for Business-Educational Partnerships.* Ottawa: Conference Board of Canada.

Boud, David. 1985. *Reflections: Turning Experiences into Learning.* London: Kegan Paul.

Bourdieu, Pierre, and J.C. Passeron. 1977. *Reproduction.* Beverley Hills: Sage.

Bowles, Samuel, and Herbert Gintis. 1976. *Schooling in Capitalist America.* New York: Basic Books.

Boyd, Monica, J. Goyder, F.E. Jones, H. McRoberts, and P.C. Pineo. 1985. *Ascription and Achievement in Canada.* Ottawa: Oxford University Press.

Breakwell, G.G., and B. Weinberger. 1986. *Young Women in Gender-Atypical Jobs: The Case of Trainee Technicians in the Engineering Industry.* Research Paper 49. London: Department of Employment.

Brethour, Patrick. 1997. "Software Firms Forced to Import Workers." Toronto, *Globe and Mail,* 20 March.

Breton, Raymond, John C. McDonald, and Stephen Richer. 1972. *Social and Economic Factors in the Career Decisions of Canadian Youth.* Ottawa: Canada Manpower and Immigration.

British Columbia Ministry of Education. 1990. *Year 2000: A Framework for Learning. Report of the Sullivan Commission.* Victoria.

Brown, C. 1984. *Black and White Britain: The Third PSI Survey.* London: Heinemann.

Brown, P. 1987. *Schooling Ordinary Kids.* London: Tavistock.

Brown, P., and D.N. Ashton, eds. 1997. *Education, Unemployment and the Labour Market.* Lewes: Falmer.

Bynner, J. 1991. "Transitions to Work: Results from a Longitudinal Study of Young People in Four British Labour Markets." In *Making Their Way: Education, Training and The Labour Markets in Canada and Britain,* edited by D.N. Ashton and G.S. Lowe. Toronto and Buckingham: University of Toronto Press/Open University Press.

Burman, Patrick. 1988. *Killing Time, Losing Ground: Experiences of Unemployment.* Toronto: Wall and Thompson.

Canada. Minister of Industry. 1996. *Reading the Future: A Portrait of Literacy in Canada.* Ottawa: Statistics Canada.

Canada Employment and Immigration Commission (CEIC). 1983. *Learning a Living. Vol. 1, Background and Perspectives, Report of the Skills Development Leave Task Force; Vol. 2, Policy Options for the Nation.* Ottawa.

– 1993. "1992 Adult Education and Training Survey." Ottawa.

– 1994A. *Learning for Life: Overcoming the Separation of Work and Learning.* Ottawa.

– 1994B. *Industry-Education Partnership Councils: Handbook for Local Action to Improve Industry-Education Cooperation.* Hamilton, ON: Industry-Education Council, Hamilton-Wentworth.

Canadian Association for Adult Education, Ian Morrison. 1995. *Adult Training in Ontario, 1991.* Toronto.

– "Analysis of the 1992 Statistics Canada Adult Education and Training Survey." With the Ontario Training and Adjustment Board. Toronto.

Canadian Education Association. 1983. *School and the Workplace: The Need for Closer Links.* Toronto.

Canadian Labour Market Productivity Centre. 1988. "The Changing Nature of the Canadian Labour Market: The Increasing Importance of Education and Training." *Quarterly Labour Market and Productivity Review: Winter,* 17–23 (Ottawa).

– 1990. *A Framework for a National Training Board.* Ottawa.

Chamie, Nicholas. 1995. *Why the Jobless Recovery?: Youth Abandon the Labour Market.* Ottawa: Conference Board of Canada.

Clarke, John, and Paul Willis. 1988. "Youth and the Transition into Adulthood." In Roger Dale, R. Ferguson, and A. Robinson. *Frameworks for Teaching.* London: Hodder and Stoughton.

Cockburn, C. 1987. *Two-Track Training: Sex Inequalities and the YTS.* London: Macmillan.

– 1979. *Schooling the Smash Street Kids.* London: Macmillan.

Coleman, James S. 1974. *Youth: Transition to Adulthood.* Panel on Youth. President's Science Advisory Committee. Washington, DC.

– 1990. *Foundations of Social Theory.* Cambridge, MA: Harvard University Press.

Collins, Randall. 1988. *Theoretical Sociology.* New York: Harcourt, Brace, Jovanovich.

Connell, R.W., D.J. Ashenden, S. Kessler, and G.W. Dowsett. 1982. *Making the Difference: Schools, Families and Social Division.* Sydney: Allen and Unwin.

Craig, M. Olsen, ed. 1988. *Industrial Change and Labour Adjustment in Sweden and Canada.* Toronto: Garamond.

Crysdale, Stewart. 1966. *Churches Where the Action Is!* Toronto: Board of Evangelism and Social Service, United Church of Canada.

– 1974A. "Secondary Education and Employment in Canada." In *Proceedings*, Conference on Education and Work, Copenhagen. Geneva: UNESCO.

– 1974B. *Power and Conflict as a Theoretical Perspective among Young Adults.* Toronto: Meetings of the International Sociological Association.

– 1979. *Individualism and Ideology among Young Adults.* In *Proceedings*, Conference on North American Values and Social Change. University of Bordeaux III.

– 1980. *The Educational and Occupational Attainment Process: A Comparative Study of Youth over Ten Years.* Annual Meeting. Canadian Sociological and Anthropological Association, Montreal, University of Quebec.

Crysdale, Stewart, and Nancy Mandell. 1993. "Gender Tracks: Male-Female Perceptions of Home-School-Work Transitions". In *Transitions: Schooling and Employment in Canada*, edited by Paul Anisef and Paul Axelrod. Toronto: Thompson Educational Publishing.

Crysdale, Stewart, and Harry MacKay. 1994. *Youth's Passage through School to Work: A Comparative, Longitudinal Study of Eastside.* Toronto: Thompson Educational Publishing.

Crysdale, Stewart, Rune Axelsson, with S. Kjellberg. 1998. "Youth's Transition to Work: Canada and Sweden." Annual Meetings of Canadian Sociology and Anthropology Association. Ottawa: University of Ottawa.

d'Amico, Ronald. 1984. "Does Employment during High School Impair Academic Progress?" *Sociology of Education* 57, no. 3 (July).

Dale, Roger, R. Ferguson, and A. Robinson. 1988. *Frameworks for Teaching.* London: Hodder and Stoughton.

Day, Diane. 1990. *Young Women in Nova Scotia.* Halifax, NS: Nova Scotia Advisory Council on the Status of Women.

Deci, E.I. 1972. *The Effects of Contingent and Noncontingent Rewards and Controls on Intrinsic Motivation.* Toronto: Toronto Board of Education.

Deem, Rosemary, ed. 1980. *Schooling for Women's Work.* London: Routledge and Kegan Paul.

Dei, George J. Sefa. 1996. *Anti-Racism Education Theory and Practice.* Halifax, NS: Fernwood Publishing.

DeVoretz, Donald, ed. 1995. *Diminishing Returns: Studies on Immigration.* Ottawa: C.D. Howe Institute, Laurier Institute.

Dex, S. 1988. "Gender and the Labour Market." In *Employment in Britain*, edited by D. Gallie. Oxford: Blackwell.

Dodge, D. 1981. *Labour Market Development in the 1980s*. Task Force on Labour Market Developments. Ottawa: Department of Employment and Immigration.

Donaldson, E.L. 1989. *Link between Education and Employment: A Case Study of Transition from School to Work*. PhD. dissertation, Ontario Institute for Studies in Education, University of Toronto.

Dransutavicius, Fiona, ed. 1988. *Partnerships in Education Resources Manual*. Hamilton, ON: Industry Education Council, Hamilton-Wentworth. Ottawa: Canada Employment and Immigration Commission.

Drohan, Madeleine. 1997. "Canada 4th Best Competitor." Report on World Economic Forum, Geneva. Toronto, *Globe and Mail*, 21 May.

Duffy, Ann, Nancy Mandell, and Norene Pupo. 1989. *Few Choices: Women, Work and Family*. Toronto: Garamond.

Economic Council of Canada. 1982. *In Short Supply: Jobs and Skills in the 1980s*. Ottawa: Economic Research Associates.

Ekos Research Associates. 1995. *Rethinking Government: A National Survey*. Toronto.

Environics Research Group. 1995. *Mood of the Nation: A Survey of Canadian Public Opinion*. Toronto.

Evers, Frederick T. 1990. *Corporate Training in Canada Survey: Summary of Results*. Guelph, ON: University of Guelph.

Faure, Edgar. 1972. *Learning to Be: The World of Education Today and Tomorrow*. International Commission on the Development of Education. Paris: UNESCO.

Finch, Michael D., M.J. Shanahan, J.T. Mortimer, and S. Ryu. 1991. "Work Experience and Control Orientation in Adolescents." *American Sociological Review* 56, no. 5 (October): 597–611.

Fleming, W.G. 1957. "Background and Personality Factors Associated with Educational and Occupational Plans of Grade 13 Students." Department of Educational Research, College of Education, University of Toronto.

Frank, Jim. 1997. *Performance and Potential 1997*. Ottawa: Conference Board of Canada.

Fredriksson, I. 1981. "Skola och arbetsliv". SOU (1981):97. *Undersokningar kring gymnasieskolan*, 97–218.

Furlong, A. 1987. *The Effects of Unemployment on the Transition to School*. Unpublished PhD thesis, University of Leicester.

Gamoran, Adam. 1992. "The Variable Effects of High School Tracking." *American Sociological Review* 57, no. 6 (December): 812–28.

Gaskell, Jane. 1977. "Stereotyping and Discrimination in the Curriculum." In *Precepts, Policy and Process*, edited by H.A. Stevenson and J.B. Wilson. London, ON: Alexander Blake Association.

Giddens, Anthony. 1979. *Central Problems in Social Theory: Action, Structure and Contradiction in Social Analysis*. London: Macmillan.

Gilbert, Sid, et al. 1993. *Leaving School: Results from a National Survey Comparing High School Leavers and Graduates 18 to 20 Years of Age*. Ottawa: Supply and Services.

Giroux, Henry. 1981. *Ideology, Culture and the Process of Schooling*. Philadelphia: Temple.

Gooderham, Mary. 1995. "Technology-Race Casualties Find They've Nowhere to Go." Toronto, *Globe and Mail*, 11 October.

Gray, J., A.F. McPherson, and D. Raffe. 1983. *Reconstructions of Secondary Education: Theory, Myth and Practice since the War*. Henley: Routledge and Kegan Paul.

Green, F., ed. 1988. *The Restructuring of the UK Economy*. Hemel Hempstead: Harvester Wheatsheaf.

Greenberger, Ellen, and Laurence D. Steinberger. 1986. *When Teenagers Work: The Psychological and Social Costs of Adolescent Employment*. New York: Basic Books.

Gzlawy, B., and J. Hudson, eds. 1996. *Youth in Transition to Adulthood: Research and Policy Implications*. Toronto: Thompson Educational Publishers.

Hall, Oswald, and Bruce McFarlane. 1962. *Transition from School to Work*. Ottawa: Department of Labour.

Hargreaves, Andy, and Michael Fullan. 1998. *What's Worth Fighting for Out There?* Toronto: Ontario Public School Teachers' Federation.

Hasan, Abrar, and P. de Broucker. 1984. "Turnover and Job Instability in Youth Labour Markets in Canada." *The Nature of Youth Unemployment*. Paris: UNESCO.

Heffren, C. 1998. *A Comparison of Literacy and Working Skills: Cooperative Education and Part-Time Jobs*. PhD, Ontario Institute for Studies in Education.

Heinemann, H.H. 1981. *Co-operative Education: Integrating Work and Learning*. Fifth International Conference on Higher Education. Lancaster, UK: University of Lancaster.

Heinz, Walter R. 1996A. "Youth Transitions in Cross-Cultural Perspective: School-Work in Germany." In *Youth in Transition to Adulthood: Research and Policy Implications*, edited by B. Gzlawy and J. Hudson. Toronto: Thompson Educational Publishers.

- 1996B. *The Transition from Education to Employment in a Comprehensive Perspective.* Toronto: Centre for International Studies, University of Toronto.

Herberg, Edward. 1982. *Ethnicity and Intergenerational Education Mobility.* Canadian Sociology and Anthropology Association, annual meeting. Ottawa.

Horwich, Herbert. 1980. "Social and Cultural Factors Affecting Retention at the Secondary and Post-Secondary Levels in Quebec." Vol. II. *Aspirations Scolaires et Orientations Professionelles des Étudiants.* Quebec: Laval University Press.

Hoskins, M., J. Sund, and D.N. Ashton. 1989. *Job Competition and Entry to Work.* Discussion Paper 111. Leicester: Department of Economics, University of Leicester.

Hruska, J. 1973. "Co-operative Education: Not for Some but for All." *Clearing House.* November.

Isajiw, Wsevolod W., A. Sev'er, and L. Driedger. 1993. "Ethnic Identity and Social Mobility: A Test of the Drawback Model." *Canadian Journal of Sociology* 18, 2 (Spring): 177–96.

Jenkins, R. 1983. *Lads, Citizens and Ordinary Kids.* London: Routledge and Kegan Paul.

Kapsalis, Constantine. 1993. "Employee Training in Canada: Reassessing the Evidence." *Canadian Business Economics* (Summer).

Karp, Ellen. 1988. *The Dropout Phenomenon in Ontario Secondary Schools.* Toronto: Ontario Ministry of Education.

Keenan, Greg. 1997. "Auto Parts Sector Warned of Shortage in Skilled Labour." Toronto, *Globe and Mail,* 24 April.

Keyfitz, Nathan. 1991. *How an Advanced Industrial Society Is Splitting into Two Nations.* Canadian Sociological and Anthropological Federation, annual meeting, June, Kingston, ON.

King, Alan J.C., and J. Hughes. 1985. *Secondary School to Work: A Difficult Transition.* Toronto: Ontario Secondary School Teachers' Association.

King, Alan, and M. Peart. 1990. *The Good School.* Toronto: Ontario Secondary School Teachers' Federation.

King, Michael, A.A. Murray, and Tom Atkinson. 1979. *Background, Personality, Job Characteristics and Satisfaction with Work in a National Sample.* Quality of Life Project, Working Paper 3. Toronto, Institute for Social Research, York University.

Kohn, Melvin L. 1976. "Occupational Structure and Alienation." *American Journal of Sociology* 82:111–30.

Kolb, Donald C. 1984. *Experiential Learning.* Englewood Cliffs, NJ: Prentice-Hall.

Krahn, Harvey, and Graham Lowe. 1991. "Transitions to Work: Findings from a Longitudinal Study of High-School and University Graduates in Three Canadian Cities." In *Making Their Way: Education Training and the Labour Market in Canada and Britain*, edited by David Ashton and Graham Lowe. Toronto: University of Toronto Press.

Lawton, Stephen B., and Kenneth A. Leithwood. 1988. *Student Retention and Transition in Ontario High Schools.* Toronto: Ontario Ministry of Education.

Lee, D., D. Marsden, P. Richmond, and J. Dunscombe. 1990. *Scheming for Youth: A Study of YTS in the Enterprise Culture.* Aldershot: Gower.

Lee, D., and J. Wrench. 1983. *Skill Seekers – Black Youth, Apprenticeships and Disadvantage.* Leicester: National Youth Bureau.

Lenski, Gerhard E. 1954. "Status Crystallization: A Non-Vertical Dimension of Social Status." *American Sociological Review* 19 (August).

Levitan, Sar A., and Frank Gallo. 1988. *A Second Chance: Training for Jobs.* Kalamazoo: W.E. Upjohn Institute for Employment Research.

Lewington, Jennifer. 1995A. "Rift Threatens Teachers' Union." Toronto, *Globe and Mail*, 9 March.

– 1995B. "School Confronts 'Big Lie' about Schools." Toronto, *Globe and Mail*, 6 October.

– 1997. "Job Training in Place." Toronto, *Globe and Mail*, 28 April.

Lgy 70. 1970. "Laroplan for gymnasieskolan 1970." *Allman del (The Upper Secondary School Curriculum). Skoloverstyrelsen.* Stockholm: Utbildningsforlaget.

Little, Bruce. 1995A. "Amazing Facts: Why It's Not So Wonderful To Be Young." Toronto, *Globe and Mail*, 9 January.

– 1995B. "Dropping Out to Find a Job? Dream On." Toronto, *Globe and Mail*, 6 November.

Little, Don. 1995. "Earnings and Labour Force Status of 1990 Graduates." *Education Quarterly Review* (Statistics Canada) 2, no. 3 (Fall).

Livingstone, D.W. 1985. *Social Crisis and Schooling.* Toronto: Garamond.

MacDonald, Madeline. 1980. "Socio-Cultural Reproduction and Women's Education". In *Schooling for Women's Work*, edited by Rosemary Deem. London: Routledge and Kegan Paul.

Mandell, Nancy. 1987. "The Family." In *An Introduction to Sociology*, edited by Michael Rosenberg. Toronto: Methuen.

Marquardt, Richard. 1996. *Youth and Work in Troubled Times: A Report on Canada in the 1990s.* Paper W01. Ottawa: Canadian Policy Networks.

Marsh, Herbert W. 1991. "Employment during High School: Character Building or a Subversion of Academic Goals." *Sociology of Education* 64, no. 3 (July): 172–89.

Meltz, Noah M. 1988. "Human Resource Management Strategies". In *Industrial Change and Labour Adjustment in Sweden and Canada*, edited by M. Olsen Craig. Toronto: Garamond.

Menzies, Heather. 1996. *Whose Brave New World.* Toronto: Between the Lines.

Morissette, René, and C. Beruben. 1994. "Recent Youth Markets in Canada: In *Recent Youth Market Experiences in Canada*, edited by Gordon Betcherman and R. Morissette. Ottawa: Statistics Canada.

Mortimer, Jeylan T., and M.D. Finch. 1986. "The Effects of Part-Time Work on Self-Concept and Achievement." In *Becoming a Worker*, edited by K. Borman and J. Reisman, Norwood, NJ: Ablex.

National Child Development Study. 1981. *Fourth Follow-up.* Working Paper 24. London: National Children's Bureau.

National Commission on the Reform of Secondary Education. 1973. *The Reform of Secondary Education: Report.* New York: McGraw-Hill.

Ninalowo, Adebayo. 1983. "Job Characteristics, Worker Affiliation and Collective Protest: A Sociological Enquiry into Labour Relations." PhD dissertation. Toronto, Department of Sociology, York University.

Olsen, Gregg, ed. 1988. *Industrial Change and Labour Adjustment.* Toronto: Garamond.

Ontario Ministry of Education. 1988. *Student Retention and Transition: Program Models.* Toronto.

Ontario. Ministry of Education and Training. 1996. *Secondary School Reform Consultation.* Toronto.

– Ministry of Skills Development. 1987. *Out of School Youth in Ontario: Their Labour Market Experience.* Toronto.

– 1989. *Pathways: A Study of Labour Market Experience and Transition Patterns of High School Leavers.* Toronto.

– Premier's Council. 1988. *Competing in the New Global Economy.* Toronto.

– 1990. *People and Skills in the New Global Economy.* Toronto.

Organization for Economic Co-operation and Development (OECD).

– 1993. *Employment Outlook.* Paris.

– 1995. *Education at a Glance, OECD Indicators.* Paris.

– 1996A. *Technology, Productivity and Job Creation.* Paris.

– 1996B. *Lifelong Learning for All.* Paris.

Peters, Suzanne. 1995. *Exploring Canadian Values.* Ottawa: Canadian Policy Research Networks.

Porter, Marion, John Porter, and Bernard Blishen. 1982. *Stations and Callings.* Toronto: Methuen.

Posterski, Donald C. 1995. *True to You: Living Our Faith in a Multi-Minded World.* Winfield, BC: Wood Lake Books.

Radwanski, George. 1987. *Ontario Study of the Relevance of Education and the Issue of Dropouts.* Toronto: Ontario Ministry of Education.

Raffe, D. 1987. "Youth Unemployment in the UK." In *Education, Unemployment and the Labour Market,* edited by P. Brown and D.N. Ashton. Lewes: Falmer.

Raffe, D., and G. Courtenay. 1988. "16–18 on both Sides of the Border." In *Education and The Youth Labour Market,* edited by D. Raffe. Lewes: Falmer.

Rawlyk, George. 1993. "God Is Alive." *Maclean's,* April 12.

Reitz, J.G. 1980. *The Survival of Ethnic Groups.* Toronto: McGraw-Hill Ryerson.

Reubens, B. 1982. "Vocational Education in Other Countries." *Education and Work.* 81st Yearbook of the National Society for the Study of Education, part 2, chapter 3, 49–70. Sweden.

Richmond, Anthony H., and W.E. Kalbach. 1980. *Factors in the Adjustment of Immigrants and Their Descendents.* Ottawa: Statistics Canada.

Riddell, W. Craig. 1995. "Human Capital Formation in Canada: Recent Developments and Policy Responses." In *Labour Market Polarization and Social Policy Reforms,* edited by K.G. Banting and C.M. Beach. Kingston, ON: School of Policy Studies, Queen's University.

Rist, Ray C., ed. 1986. *Finding Work: Cross-National Perspectives on Employment and Training.* Philadelphia: Palmer Press.

Roberts, K., S. Dench, and D. Richardson. 1986. *The Changing Structure of Youth Labour Markets.* Research Paper 59. London: Department of Employment.

Rokeach, Milton. 1973. *The Nature of Human Values.* New York: Free Press.

Rosenbaum, James E. 1996. "Policy Uses of Research on Transition." *Sociology of Education* extra issue, 102–22.

Rosenbaum, James E., and Takehiko Kariya. 1991. "Do School Achievements Affect the Early Jobs of High School Graduates in the United States and Japan?" *Sociology of Education* 64, no. 2 (April): 78–95.

Rosenberg, Michael, ed. 1987. *An Introduction to Sociology.* Toronto: Methuen.

Royster, Deirdre A. 1997. "Racial Variations in the Influence of Institutional and Social Networks on the School-to-Work Transition: Evidence from a Case Study." Paper presented at the annual meeting of the American Sociological Association, August, Toronto.

Ryrie, Alexander C. 1983. *On Leaving School.* Edinburgh: Scottish Council for Research into Education.

Sewell, William H. 1970. "The Educational and Early Occupational Attainment Process: Replication and Revision." *American Sociological Review* 35, no. 6 (December): 1,014–27.

Simon, Roger. 1991. *Learning to Work.* New York: Bergin and Garvey.

Slavin, Robert E. 1990. *Co-operative Learning: Theory, Research and Practice.* Englewood Cliffs, NJ: Prentice-Hall.

Smart, Carol. 1990. "The Legal and Moral Ordering of Child Custody." Unpublished paper. Warwick, UK, Department of Sociology, University of Warwick.

SOU 1986: 2. (Swedish Government Official Reports). *En trearig yrkesutbildning. Del 1. Riktlinjer for fortsatt arbete (A Three-Year Upper Secondary Vocational Education). Betankande av expertgruppen for oversyn av den gymnasiala yrkesutbildningen* (OGY). Stockholm: Utbildningsdepartementet.

Spain, W.H., D.B. Sharpe, and Andrea Maudle. 1991. *Life after High School: A Profile of Early Leavers in Newfoundland.* St John's, NF, Centre for Educational Research, Memorial University.

Squires, Robert J. 1995. *R and D Outlook for 1995.* Ottawa: Conference Board of Canada.

Starr, Laura. 1987. "The Transition from School to Work: Socialization through Role Continuity." Unpublished paper, Department of Education, Hebrew University of Jerusalem.

Statistics Canada. 1989. *Canada's Youth: A Profile of Their Labour Market Experience. 1986.* Ottawa: Labour and Household Surveys Analysis Division.

– 1991. *Changing Faces: Visible Minorities in Toronto.* Ottawa.

– 1994A. *Women in the Labour Force.* Ottawa.

– 1994B. *Canada's Changing Immigrant Populations.* Ottawa.

– 1996. "Initial Results of School Leavers' Followup Study." *Education Quarterly Review* 3, no. 4. (Winter): n.p. Catalogue 81–083-XPB.

– 1997. *The Labour Force.* January. Catalogue 71–001.

Stern, David, Thomas Bailey, and Donna Merritt. 1997. *School-to-Work Policy Insights from Recent International Developments.* Berkeley: National Centre for Research in Vocational Education, University of California at Berkeley.

Sunter, Deborah. 1993. *School, Work and Dropping Out: Perspectives on Labour and Income.* Catalogue 75–001E. Ottawa: Statistics Canada.

– 1994. *Youth – Waiting It Out: Perspectives on Labour and Income.* Catalogue 75–001E. Ottawa: Statistics Canada.

Tanner, J., H. Krann, and T.H. Hartnagel. 1995. *Fractured Transition from School to Work: Revisiting the Dropout Problem.* Toronto: Oxford University Press.

Thomas, Alan M. 1989. *The Utilization of Prior Learning Assessment as a Basis for Admission and Advanced Standing in Education in Canada.* Toronto: Ontario Institute for Studies in Education.

Thomas, D.L. 1974. *Family Socialization and the Adolescent: Determinants of Self-Concept, Conformity, Religiosity and Countercultural Values.* Lexington, MA: Lexington Books.

Tully, D. Blair. 1988. "Ontario's New Training Strategy." In *Industrial Change and Labour Adjustment,* edited by Gregg M. Olsen. Toronto: Garamond.

United States General Accounting Office. 1990. *Training Strategies: Preparing Noncollege Youth for Employment in the US and Foreign Countries.* Washington, DC.

Walker, Stephen, and Len Barton. 1983. *Gender, Class and Education.* London: Falmer Press.

Wallace, C. 1987. *For Richer: For Poorer.* London: Tavistock.

Wallin, E., and R. Axelsson. 1982. "An Evaluation of Swedish Upper Secondary Education-Project UTGY." Paper presented at the eighth annual conference of the International Association of Educational Assessment, May, Sodertalje, Sweden.

Weber, Max. 1958. *From Max Weber.* Translated by H.H. Gerth and C. Wright Mills. New York: Oxford University Press.

Weiss, Lois. 1990. *Working Class without Work.* New York: Routledge.

Wells, Amy, and Jennie Oakes. 1996. "Potential Pitfalls of Systematic Reform: Lessons from Detracting Research." *Sociology of Education* extra issue, 135-43.

Wenglinsky, Harold. 1997. "How Money Matters: Effect of School Spending on Academic Achievement." *Sociology of Education* 70, no. 3 (July): 221-37.

West, M.P. Newton. 1983. *The Transition from School to Work.* Beckenham: Croom Helm.

William T. Grant Foundation. 1988. *The Forgotten Half: Pathways to Success for American Youth and Young Families.* Washington, DC: Commission on Work, Family and Citizenship.

Willis, P. 1977. *Learning to Labour.* Farnborough: Saxon House.

Woelfel, Joseph, and A.E. Haller. 1971. "Significant Others, the Self-Reflective Act and the Attitude Formation Process." *American Sociological Review* 36 (February): n.p.

Young, Vivienne, and Carol Reich. 1974. *Patterns of Dropping Out.* Toronto Board of Education.

Index

Entries to citations are under the name of the first author